The Ideal Dog

Also by Tom Henry

The Good Company: An Affectionate
History of the Union Steamships
Paul Bunyan on the West Coast
Dogless in Metchosin

The Ideal Dog
and Other Delusions

Tom Henry

Illustrations by
Greta Guzek

Harbour
Publishing

HARBOUR PUBLISHING
P.O. Box 219
Madeira Park, BC V0N 2H0 Canada

Most stories in this collection were broadcast, in somewhat
different form, on CBC Radio. "Welcome to the Bone Yard"
was first published in *Western Living*.

Cover painting and interior graphics by Greta Guzek.
Cover design by Roger Handling/Terra Firma.
Page design and composition by David Lee Communications.

Printed and bound in Canada

Canadian Cataloguing in Publication Data

Henry, Tom, 1961–
  The ideal dog and other delusions

  ISBN 1-55017-150-X

  1. Country Life—British Columbia—Metchosin (District)—Anecdotes. 2.
Country life—British Columbia—Metchosin (District)—Humor. 3. Canadian
wit and humor (English)* I. Title.
PS8565.E645I33 1996   C818'.5402   C96-910489-8
PR9199.3.H455I33 1996

Acknowledgements

For their thoughtful editorial suggestions I am indebted to David Gullason and Hardeep Dhaliwal, both of the CBC, and to Mary Schendlinger of Harbour Publishing. Stories in this collection also benefited from the wise eye and good heart of Lorna Jackson.

Table of Contents

Part Three
Seed Time

Part Four
Dog Days

Welcome to the Bone Yard

Behind our cabin, between the chicken coop and the wood-shed, is a rocky, oil-blackened patch of ground approximately the size of a two-car garage. It is tufted with grass around the edges so it resembles a monk's tonsure, and it is home to a variety of tools: the chain saws and chopping block, the axes (one for falling, two for splitting), assorted oil and gas tanks, a peavey, 150 feet of blue 2-inch polyester line, coiled, plus a half dozen potato plants, holidaying volunteers from the nearby compost. Every farm has an area like this one. Since Lorna and I and our five-year-old daughter Lily moved here four years ago, we've called ours the bone yard.

The bone yard is where the chickens are beheaded, where the gnarly, knotted chunks of wood that resist splitting are laid up for further study. It's where kids slip away to do bad things to the cat, where dads wander to pee, smoke and think about what to do with those kids. It is, in the broadest sense, a working area.

I like the bone yard. I go there every morning. Lily and I get up at 6:30 and I make her toast with peanut butter and cut off the crusts. Then I carry the crusts to the chickens. While they scurry about, I perch on the splitting block and listen. Chicken squawks and thrush songs on one side, toilet flushes and toy truck sounds on the other. It's an outdoor version of the music lover's "sweet spot," that point in a hall where the sounds meet in equilibrium.

I also write from the bone yard. It works like this. When I feed the chickens I see my axes. The axes remind me of cutting firewood, which I do for several months every fall, for a land-owner named Wayne. For each cord I cut, Wayne pays me $60. Last time I worked for Wayne, he and I had lunch, on a stump, in the rain. As the water matted our hair and softened our sandwiches he told me about an old farmer who had died recently. The farmer had doubled as the local livestock slaugh-terer, and on his deathbed he had grasped his wife's hand with his bony fingers and said, "Thank God for one thing. I'm not going to have to kill any more animals."

You won't find material like that in a library. I would have cut two cords to get that story. The money was just a perk.

Behind the axes, in an unpainted plywood toolbox, is an empty plastic vinegar bottle. I fill it with drinking water and take it with me when I work. One of my first jobs after moving to Metchosin was haying. Every day and all day from mid-May to the end of June I pitched bales from field to wagon, wagon to barn. It was simple work, done in open fields in the sunshine. Between loads I would take long drafts of water from the vinegar bottle, always taking care to pour some in my hand for the farm dog, a Dalmatian–Lab bitch named Sam—whose company I appreciated all the more because our landlord does not permit us to have a dog.

That water was so good, and Sam and I enjoyed it so deeply, I could not stop thinking about it. Even after work, while I was lying on my living room couch, too exhausted to strip off my sweat-stained work clothes, water coursed through my mind. One night after haying, I made some notes on foolscap about water, and work, and Sam. I put the notes together and sent them to a Vancouver newspaper. The newspaper published the story on a Saturday. On Tuesday a CBC Radio producer phoned. Would I be interested in doing a short series of similar pieces for broadcast? The producer suggested I do one story a week for several weeks. I said sure. That series, known as CBC's Country Life column, ran for three years and yielded two books, the second of which you hold in your hands. The vinegar bottle is my reservoir.

The bone yard also reminds me of the way I don't want to write. Before moving to the country I lived in Victoria. I worked for a zealous city magazine, covering, among other beats, the legislature. I zipped about, buglike, with a hand-held tape recorder thrust out at arm's length. I worried nonstop about the batteries in the tape recorder running low. I wore a tie and striped shirts manufactured from material that made me stink. After two years of less-than-zealous performance, I was fired. Lorna and I rented a moving truck with a hole in the muffler and moved to Metchosin. I promised myself I would never again write a serious word about politics.

Then, one night during the last municipal election, a friend knocked at my door. Was I interested in some writing work? We got in his truck and drove to a neighbour's home. The neighbour is a developer. Around this community, perched on the fast-metastasizing edges of Greater Victoria, developers are regarded with an enthusiasm usually reserved for anthrax or root rot. This developer, an acquaintance of my friend's, was running for local council. He wanted me to write out the lumps in the wording of his pitch. Normally I would have rejected such work. But there I was, in another man's kitchen, eating his cookies, listening to his wife laughing with their son. It seemed to me we already had a compact, if not an actual contract. Furthermore, I had ducked last month's rent, and prospects for achieving the next month's rent were poor. Circumstances had massed against me. I pulled a pen from my pocket and set to work.

The next day, while lying on my back in the bone yard and greasing my truck, I wondered what the hell had got into me. I wasn't just writing about politics, I was writing politics. The rocks in my back and the grit falling in my eyes were hard reminders, like a teacher's swat across the head, of what I should—and shouldn't—be doing.

About halfway along the length of the bone yard the ground breaks away to a fern-strewn ravine. Clumps of grass grow thick and high, forming a green shag dense enough to conceal hen's eggs, screwdrivers, a child's favourite golf ball. It's healthy in a rough, true sort of way. There is no distinction between nature and man, no false dichotomies.

This, for me, is the most important aspect of the bone yard. Truth is a maligned concept, but I believe (perhaps innocently) it has a resonance, a sweet spot hard to find and impossible to counterfeit. A writer may describe brilliantly (for example) the Malaysian rain forests, but until she tells me how it felt to bark her shin on a jungle hardwood, or defecate among the foliage, her work will always ring of tin. I wonder: who was in that jungle anyway—a tape recorder, or a living, breathing, crapping person?

True writing is rare. I've found it in the books of Roderick Haig-Brown, a leather-skinned, beak-nosed Englishman who moved to Campbell River in the early part of this century. Haig-Brown took as his inspiration the natural history of West Coast streams and rivers, and the salmon that inhabit them. He wrote forthrightly and beautifully about hunting and fishing. He was a master with a fly rod and with the English language; his sentences reel and flow with semicolons and cadences. His words sound good.

At one time I attempted to write facsimiles of Haig-Brown's work. I clipped a picture of him from an old magazine and tacked it to the wall above my desk. In the picture, Haig-Brown was seated in a high-backed chair in his study, sucking a pipe and looking thoughtfully out the window at the Campbell River. I would sit in my chair, look at the picture and try to have the same thoughts, complete with semicolons. I even flirted with a pipe, hoping the sucking action might jump-start the style. It didn't; my stories were as dry and unpalatable as wind-burned hay.

The picture now resides in a bottom drawer. I'd be lost in a high-backed chair. There's only one place that lets me know where I am: between the chicken coop and the woodshed.

Welcome to the bone yard.

Part One

Fall of the Leaf

Chicken Leg, Dog Leg

To get to our house you take the highway north out of Victoria, turn right onto a secondary, then a left, follow that road until you get to Chuck's (the general store), make a dog leg, keep on that road until it splits, hang right, sharp left down our lane, ignore the sign saying "Stop! No trespassing!," second driveway and watch out for our chickens. And one more thing: back down the drive, because there's no place in our yard to turn around.

Right, left, right, right, dog leg, chicken leg, reverse—no wonder we don't have many guests. A friend visiting from the city said getting to our place was like slithering into a crawl space. Once he was here all he could think about was how he was going to get out.

Lorna, Lily and I have lived in this cabin for four years. You might think that by now we would have devised a smooth and easy-to-follow set of instructions to guide people to our doorstep. But no.

It seems to me the country resident has few choices when it comes to issuing directions. Either you can give up on guests altogether—and do away with the need for directions—or you can try to issue directions in a palatable form. Being a reluctantly social family, we do the latter. We are able to guide visitors as far as Chuck's, but then everything falls apart. I think it has something to do with the word "Chuck." "Chuck" is over-familiar, and suggests to potential guests that a visit with Chuck and his staff is a prerequisite for a visit with us.

And it's not only the right turn at Chuck's that gets our visitors. A little farther along, there is another checkpoint: a very small field beside the road to our house, which is home to two enormous fat dirty ewes.

"Watch for the sheep," I tell people, right after I mention the sharp left.

"Sheep?" They respond as if I have suggested they use a fast-travelling layer of alto-cirrus cloud as a landmark. In fact, sheep—as a species, or as a lonely pair in a small field—cannot be said to move in any meaningful way. Empires and hair styles come and go, but those two sheep remain.

Between Morgan's Hill and Spanky's barn, that same road to our house dipsy-doodles near the ocean. This too throws visitors. They see water and think they have overshot our home. So we tell them to watch for the donkey farm, which has a sign: "Spotted Asses." Soon after we moved to this cabin, I phoned my father to give him directions. Watch for the Spotted Asses sign, I said. Dad replied he already knew the way to the municipal hall, it was directions to my place he needed.

Sometimes I think I'd like to give up on the guest thing, and the directions that go with it. That's what the Olsens did. The Olsens owned several thousand acres of wheat field and range in Groundbirch, in northern BC, where my parents had a grain farm. They enjoyed the company of our family and the local store owner, but otherwise they were their own best friends. One day their eldest son, my friend Chris, and I were walking the local gravel road when a large pickup with Wisconsin licence plates pulled up beside us. Inside were two American hunters, with big guns and many beer.

"Hey boys," one of them drawled, "know where we can find the Olsen spread?" Old Man Olsen was a superb hunter, and had a wide reputation as a knowledgeable woodsman.

I hesitated; Chris did not.

"Sure, sure I know," he said, peering far down the road. "See that hill? Go a couple miles past, turn south, follow the road, through three gates, four gates and keep on. Their spread is up there."

Chris's directions sounded so authentic, with jabs of the thumb left and right, that I almost believed him myself. Except that we were actually right in front of the Olsens' home at the time, and that clanging emanating from the garage behind us was likely Old Man Olsen himself taking yet another round out of his recalcitrant John Deere tractor.

The Yanks left in a spray of gravel. A left and three or four gates—that would put them square into the community pasture, a zillion acres of bush and grassland. I still wonder if a well-preserved pickup isn't sitting out there, with two skeletons in it, clutching beer cans.

Chris and I watched the truck disappear, then wandered into the shop.

"What did those fellas want?" asked Old Man Olsen, wrench in hand.

"Looking for you," said Chris. "But I just told them to get lost."

Critters

Of all the great migrations occurring in October—salmon, turkey vultures, monarch butterflies—the migration that impresses me most is the one going on in our own yard. In the seven days since it turned cold, scores of bugs and animals have moved deliberately and swiftly from bush and lawn to the wood-heated warmth of our cabin. Big, small, hairy. Four-legged, eight-legged. They've transformed our three-person, one-cat shack into a crowded multi-species ark.

Every society, human or otherwise, has a hierarchy, and the mixed society in our cabin is no exception. At the top are the spiders. Spiders are the aristocrats of the bug world. They fare well on others' mistakes, and have long legs. They have webbed in every corner of our house, low and high, in every room, every window sill. There is a small spider in the tooth-brush drawer in the little bathroom, and a big one somewhere in my closet. We even have a seven-legged spider. It lives under the right-hand side of the window couch—wisely, since that's where Lily eats her toast in the mornings and there are crumbs aplenty. This spider comes out at 10:00 every night, looking like a Civil War veteran, to warm itself by the stove. I took a jab at it once with the broom, and it actually came toward me, boldly. Since then we've had a rough peace.

At the other end of the social scale are the voles. Or, as we call them, snackers. Snackers are so numerous under the porch at this time of the year that our cat can step out the door and have one in the time it takes me to make a peanut butter and raisin sandwich. She kills more than she can eat and leaves their crushed bodies on the deck, bony doormats for us to step on in the morning.

Somewhere in the middle of this class system are the mice. I like mice, but only in principle, not in my house. They carry diseases, just as rats do. I trap them or shut them into a room with poisoned bait, and keep a tally of my kills.

Still, I have sympathy for one mouse, who has returned to this cabin every autumn for at least three years. He may predate us. He winters under the house and annexes the kitchen behind the stove. He stays there if the stove is warm and, we suspect, has sex partners over to visit. Late at night we hear vigorous thrashing amid the metal pie plates. We are never quick enough to catch him, in or out of the act.

One evening last fall we were reading in the living room when we heard a telltale clang from under the stove. Moments later Lorna spotted a mouse slipping through one of the doorways to our kitchen, likely bound for a healthy chunk of cookie on the floor. The mouse did not scurry, she said, it strolled, and tucked in under the stereo.

Now, a nervous, sneaky mouse is one thing, but a cocky mouse in the living room? It was an affront to our domestic security, like a late-night phone call from a telemarketer.

Immediately I sicced the cat on the mouse, but the cat was asleep, belly stuffed with snackers.

So I got up, book in hand, and motioned Lorna to do the same. She would go to one side of the stereo, me on the other. When the mouse came out—*wham!* or *squish!* or whatever happens when you hit a mouse with a hardcover.

Lorna leaned down; I leaned down. We closed in and—*squirt!* that mouse shot out on my side, bounding like a race horse. It flashed past the cookie, and past another mouse that was now feasting on the cookie, and both mice vanished into the kitchen. We'd been done, in a critter version of the give-and-go play.

I know. Such talk is anthropomorphic. But to anyone who doubts the intelligence of mice, or of any of the other animals living in our shack, let me say this. It is impossible not to think of them as intelligent when, in the middle of rainy season, they move into a wood-heated, carpeted home with an electric stove and homemade cookie crumbs. The critters in our ark have far more than just the animal sense to migrate out of the rain.

Make Dirt, Not War

If I were to strip our home economy into components and set them out on the barn floor for inspection, the first and most important items would be our composters. We have: a black plastic tower composter, which looks like the Pickering nuclear station, on the east side of the house; a wooden box composter behind the garage; two composters for leaves up in the bush; and a wire mesh composter near the cow field. For consistently fine production, the kitchen composter is best, though when we load up the one near the field with fresh cow pies and chicken manure, it produces a black earthy brew that does to plants what growth hormones do to swine.

The composters are, in a literal sense, the First Cause in our domestic economy. No compost, no soil; no soil, no garden; no garden...no reason to be here. Even if we were content to survive on store-bought foods, which we are not, we'd be lost without our composters. The soil they produce fuels vines, flowers, shrubs—all the things that make this "our home," as distinct from yet another rented shack.

I enjoy composting. It is one of the few satisfying things you can do that does not require an erection or a credit card. It is slow, which is good discipline for those of us who like to achieve our pleasures swiftly. Composting opens out into one of those broad concepts that is a metaphor for everything. Given enough time to sit and rot, even bum relationships and ugly family episodes are rendered fecund: sad to happy, dysfunctional to functional. All you need is time and warmth.

Lorna and I consider ourselves Adult Children of Composters, though compared to me she is hard-core. I trace my enthusiasm to my teenage years in Duncan, when rich kids from Queen Margaret's private school would clop their horses past my parents' place. Whenever a horse pooped, my mom zoomed out with a shovel, eager for compost fodder. When I objected, and said scooping poop was a demeaning thing for a grown woman to do, she said "You're right," and delegated it to me.

Talk about your metaphor. After scooping up rich kids' horse poop for a few months, I understood exactly what the French Revolution had been about. "Let them eat humus."

Lorna's composting antecedents are less political. As a young girl in Vancouver's comfy Kerrisdale area, she one day discovered a potato growing amid the backyard grass clippings. She dug for more, and has never stopped digging. She has had composters in every place she's lived, including one on a ranch in 100 Mile House that I'm still not ready to talk about. When I met Lorna, she even had a compost in her apartment, making do with the produce compartment in her fridge.

Lorna makes better compost than me. She makes more compost than me. Her compost, unlike mine, does not contain cigarette butts, or tinfoil. At one time I was jealous of these qualities. Then, two years ago, I realized Lorna's talents were an opportunity, not a challenge. For Christmas that year I gave her the black plastic composter, and got a friend of hers to give her a compost turner, a long, surgical-looking doodad. Both gifts flew. I've since endeared myself to her with wheelbarrow loads of manure from our chicken coop and rabbit hutch. And I'm discovering new ways of endearing myself all the time.

Several weeks ago Lorna and I were in the garden when she hoisted the little door at the bottom of her composter, as she periodically does. Out poured an oily black mix, alive with squirming young worms, good enough to eat. Or so she claimed.

"You know," I said, "if you die before me, I'm going to put you in the composter, then spread you all over the garden."

I might as well have peeled a fresh onion under her nose.

"Aw," she sniffed, "that's the nicest thing you've ever said to me."

My Brother Hugh

I come from a family of five siblings. Four of us live in the country: Beth, who is married to a logger, has a house on the side of a mountain in the Cowichan Valley; Guy's place is on a large property in Westholme, near Chemainus; Paul is in the Yukon; I'm in Metchosin.

Then there is Hugh. Brother Hugh lives on the third floor of a brick and stucco apartment block at the confluence of two busy streets in Duncan. The rest of us, to varying degrees, enjoy hard physical work; Hugh, to all degrees, hates hard work. He says he'd rather pick up a slug with his bare hands than grasp anything with a wood handle. He is large, unmuscular, fond of mornings spent watching NFL football and munching on tuna and Miracle Whip sandwiches. In short, he's a perfect definition of the type of person who should not live in the country.

Yet I've always thought that if I were to do the pioneer thing—to march into the bush and construct a cabin and fend for myself—I'd take Hugh along. I might have to discard the double-headed axe to help him across a creek, and empty my rucksack of provisions to make way for his cigarettes, but it would be worth it.

Hugh, unlike others in my family, was born with the understanding that muscle and toughness are not assets but impediments. And that is an advantage. The temptation to use brawn instead of brain is overwhelming in the country, where there is always something to split, to heave, to grunt up or down. My family is still loath to talk about the time, years back, when the shaft fell off the Allis Chalmers crawler. While the rest of us were snorting and using our fingers for pry bars, Hugh quietly rigged up a come-along and a sling. The shaft slid painlessly into place. It was embarrassing, really, which is probably why Mom and Dad hustled him off to university the next year.

I live in the country, not the bush, but Hugh's talents still come in handy. One early fall evening, Hugh, Lily and I were driving home from a party in Duncan. The party was a family affair, with a bathtub full of soft drinks and beer, loud music, aggressive croquet, and just enough wafting fumes from the overtaxed septic system to keep everything earthy. In short, a fine country party.

My truck is small. Hugh is big. While Lily curled up in the passenger seat, Hugh crawled into the truck box under the canopy and sat with his back against the cab. As we wound our home way along a back road I was overwhelmed with the pleasantness, the goodness, of the evening. Here a dead raccoon in the road, there a Stilton-coloured waxing moon. The headlights caught the mountain shapes of cows in passing fields. I was especially pleased with the thought of having a brother in the back, like a spare tire, and wished momentarily he could stay there forever.

Hugh had suggested we pick up some beer on the way home, then drink it after Lily was tucked in. As we pulled in to the cold beer store, I noticed a pickup truck in the middle of the parking lot. Leaning against the truck was a young man, pissing. It was such a good night—such a great night—that even this sight was beautiful, in a rural Duncan sort of way, and I jokingly commented to the fellow as we parked that from the looks of things, it was mighty chilly out.

It was a thoughtless, provoking comment, I now realize.

"How about you get a taste of my biceps?" the fellow barked.

I'm not against fist fights—I've fought before and I'll probably do it again, especially if I don't get paid for that ditch-digging I did last month—but I didn't want to scrap in front of my daughter. The fellow hollered again and I got out of the truck. He was puffed up like a rooster, trying to make himself look large and terrible. What to do? To me it seemed the options were two: fight or flight. But that was me; Hugh had other ideas. The tailgate popped down and he unfolded from the truck, slowly. He kept coming out and coming out, like he was twenty-two feet tall. And when he stood, he kept going up. Up. Up. Up. "Wow," I thought. "What a big brother I have!" I could have cheered, but that would have given us away.

The young fellow looked at Hugh, paused, said something like "Next time, jerk" and left in a shriek of squealing tires.

"Any time!" I called bravely.

My brother Hugh may be allergic to axe handles and hard work, but he's got a few tricks that make the rest of us look like apartment dwellers.

The Ideal Dog

If the landlord permitted me to own a dog, I'd have a dog with a trailer hitch. A silver hitch, so it would take a shine. I have lived on farms with dogs before. The injustice of a dog freelancing around while you dig post holes is the injustice of a Whistler jet-setter and a hard-working gas jockey. With a trailer hitch, my dog could pull his own weight—plus a wagon full of firewood.

My dog, my *ideal* dog, would also have the following qualities: he (or she) would be assertive, cocky, persistent, affectionate, full of bravado and blessed with a terrific sense of humour. He would stick his tongue out, and not just when he was hot.

Those descriptions, incidentally, come from the chapter on five-year-olds in one of our child care books. The only real difference between the ideal kid and the ideal dog is that dogs have that funny toenail a third of the way up their leg while kids have a toenail in their mouth. Still, you want both to be happy and healthy, and to ride around with you in the truck.

My dog would also be a Liberal. Liberals are really left- and right-wingers who have rolled in the stench of convenience, and a dog that was a Liberal wouldn't have to seek out a rotten deer carcass to mask his natural odours. Besides, if a dog was a Liberal I wouldn't feel bad about getting him fixed.

My dog would be big—nothing less than a Lab. At one time I would have wished for a smaller dog, but that was when I was younger, and masculinity oozed out of me like sap from a fir stump. Now that I have turned thirty-five, and the sap is ebbing, a large dog would supplement the loss. Like a toupee for disappearing hormones.

A farm dog, unlike a residential dog, actually has to work. One task I'd assign the dog would be frightening off the otters that calve under the outbuildings. Whew! Speaking of Liberals. In accomplishing this task, the dog would be aided if he could co-operate with a cat. This sounds like an unusual partnership, until you understand that dog–cat animosity is an urban conceit, a luxury born of too little to do. In the country, dogs and cats have to work together. Dave, my landlord, once had a dog that teamed up with an ochre-coloured tom to hunt otter. While the otter bit one, the other bit the otter. Afterwards, cat and dog snoozed on the porch, curled together like the I Ching.

My dog, my ideal dog, wouldn't have ear mites. He would be easy on kids and hard on building inspectors. He wouldn't bark often, but when he did, they would be deep, meaningful barks. He would slip on his own leash when the landlord came sniffing around, then falsely strain at it.

He would also be savvy. Savvy means that when we had a guest the dog would ensure their visit was enjoyable and brief: enjoyable for the dog, brief for the guest. I know a dog like this.

The Ideal Dog

He lives with a bookish couple on the Sunshine Coast. When you arrive, Rocky throws himself on his back and his hind foot spins in anticipation of long belly rubs. He slobbers at the thought of endless ball chasing. He does not leave you alone. At night he climbs into the small guest bed, then turns diagonally. At all times, a part of his body must be touching a part of your body. If you shift away in your slumbers, he growls. After one night you are so doggy, you cut short the visit and leave. Which makes you the ideal guest.

The landlord says the ideal dog doesn't exist. He says dogs dig deep in the flower garden. He says they chase sheep, attract cougars and chew on the house. He says the ideal dog is a delusion. That is understandable. Dave has never lived without a dog. Only the truly dogless appreciate just how ideal a dog can be.

Crash Course in Chicken Lore

If you're looking for a quick fix of farm lore, in the collected fact and fancy of rural life, you should buy chickens. Lore comes with a flock, and so do mites, strong manure and sun-yellow eggs.

We've had our new flock for ten days. We got them to supplement our old flock, which had been reduced by hawks and raccoons to just three: two egg-layers, and an indolent old hen named Bridget. We were told we should kill Bridget, as it was a known fact among farmers that a lazy chicken sets a bad example. But I kept her, in part because she was beautiful, in part because no matter how late I slept, Bridget was still snoozing in the coop. She made me feel good.

Still, two eggs a day isn't enough to feed us, let alone sell and pay for hen scratch. We started asking around about the wisdom of adding younger birds to our flock. Here is what I was told in a single morning. At the small hobby farm of a neighbour: "Can't do it. Old birds will peck the young ones to death. Got to kill the old ones off." Two hours later, in the kitchen of a retired farm wife: "No problem. The idea that a new flock won't work with an old flock is from one of those how-to books. Don't let your chickens read the books, and you'll be fine."

I'm all for literacy, but I'm for old chickens too. We decided to try melding flocks.

I phoned the farmer who had sold us our original flock and inquired about new chickens. Yes, he said, he'd just had four hundred shipped in. This was good news. I had also been told—lorelike—that suppliers order young chickens in large volumes and the first customers get the pick of the litter. I wanted a half dozen; out of four hundred I should be able to get the very best.

I wonder if the person who coined the phrase "pick of the litter" has ever tried catching the six best birds out of a flock of four hundred? I wonder if they've ever inhaled that lovely combination of sawdust and dried chickenshit that stings the eyes and clogs the nostrils? Four hundred excited chickens in a confined barn raise a thick fog, and as the farmer and I blundered around, arms and legs spread wide, I was reminded of how difficult it was to get a dance partner in Grade Nine. To make matters worse, the farmer was a devout Christian and I am not, and my chicken-catching language upset him deeply. What I ended up with, I now believe, was six wimpy chickens— because they were the easiest ones to catch.

We brought the chickens home and released them into the pen. As a precaution against pecking, and on the sage advice of yet another neighbour, I'd divided the coop in two with chicken wire. That way the flocks could see each other, and safely establish an order of sorts. As instructed, I left the wire up for three days. On the fourth day I took the wire down and… and one of the veteran chickens flew over and pecked a new chicken. Then pecked her again and again, until I booted her out of the way. So much for sage advice.

I was told some time ago about an old-fashioned solution for troublesome chickens. It came from a bass-voiced Dane, once reported to have been the strongest man at the Chemainus sawmill. "Take de chicken and pud id in jail," he said. By jail he meant an upside-down garbage bucket. Standard sentence: forty-eight hours; slightly more for egg eating, slightly less for sexual deviancy. After two days and nights of facing its own minuscule thoughts, the chicken emerges only too eager to integrate with the flock.

So we put our errant chicken "in jail." I didn't keep it under the bucket for a full two days, I'll admit now, because I felt obliged to give it the mandatory one third off for good behaviour. I was also worried that the treatment might work. I'm a bit of a lefty liberal, and I hate it when heavy-handed, right-wing prescriptions actually work, in or out of the farmyard.

I needn't have worried. I hoisted the garbage pail and instead of a chastened and reformed chicken running out, as predicted, several other chickens scurried over and gave it a pecking.

If that doesn't tell you something about lore, then I've got a heck of a deal on a flock of garbage buckets.

More Than Plenty

I associate months of the year with colours, just as I associate them with different foods. August is the deep green of mature foliage; September the brush-cut blond of parched hay fields; October is the ochre of dead and dying maple leaves.

Our cabin is walled in on the east side by a stand of broadleaf maples. In summer the greenery on these trees is so thick it dampens vehicle sounds on the landlord's lane, so we are unable to distinguish, as we usually can, pickup from pickup, car from car. Come late autumn, however, this wall falls away, leaf by leaf, and we regain sights and sounds to the east.

Right now, from where I stand in the bone yard, I can look through those leafless maples to a bright splotch of orange on the hillside. That splotch is my chain saw. It's a Husqvarna with a thirty-two-inch bar. The saw is old, having done time with a falling contractor up coast, then with my nephew, also a logger, then me. In the last two years I've cut over two hundred cords with it. A week ago I started cutting wood for next year, and left the saw on the bank, along with my gas and oil, axes and wedges.

The saw has certain associations for me. Pain in my lower back, deep singsong ringing in my ears, cash. For several years that saw pulled Lorna, Lily and me through lean autumns. We were bust, and I remember, with an egg-sized lump in my throat, how I felt whenever it coughed or misbehaved.

"Come on," I'd plead, pulling on the starter cord. "Come on. Oh please, please start." Enough pulls and it would go. That saw has done more for my spirituality than all my Sunday school teachers combined.

The Husqvarna is the latest of many saws I've owned. My first was a little Dolmar that I bought when I was sixteen and carried around in a black case, like a gangster. My friends and I used that saw for cutting wood on weekends for beer money. We didn't have our own timber so, as one of my friends, who was the son of a lawyer, put it, we were "forced" to steal the wood. The best time to do this is early morning. I'd get up, drive my truck to the lawyer's house, and honk the horn. My friend, who liked to sleep in, would eat his fried eggs and bacon in the truck. As we bounced along back roads, looking for trees with a roadward lean, the fried eggs would slither onto his lap. "Don't worry about a thing," he'd say, scooping up the mess. "Find the tree, cut it up, get it on the truck. Possession is nine-tenths of the law. Besides, Dad will take care of the other tenth."

Other saws: a Stihl, which wouldn't run, and which broke the toe of a buddy who tried, literally, to kick-start it; a plastic Jonsereds that I demolished while falling a cedar in Glenora;

a Pioneer that is now, properly, at the bottom of Lake Cowichan.

Most of all, however, I associate chain saws with people. Wood cutting, like much nakedly physical work, is a social activity that masquerades as a solitary act. You work alone, but in close proximity to others. Just the other day, my parents came to visit Lily while I set to work cutting the maples. My intention was to take the full day and buck and haul two cords of firewood. Never mind the splitting and stacking, Lily and I could do that later. I started at 8:30. At 10:30 I saw my father picking his way up the hill, a shiny object in each hand. My father is often thirsty, and he detects thirst in others. The beer was cold. We perched on stumps and drank it. We saw an enormous indigo beetle. We talked comfortably about Wendell Berry and Louis Bromfield—things we have talked about before. When we finished the beer, it was time to head to the cabin for lunch, and after lunch we decided to drive to East Sooke and look for turkey vultures kettling. I cut a half cord, maybe. Not enough to heat the cabin, but on some days nothing is more than plenty. The saws wait.

Dignity on a Dirty Job

Of all the people I've worked with—office clerks, newspaper reporters, farmhands—the most independent-minded are workers in the resource industries. Loggers, miners, fishermen. It's as if they live in the highball 1950s, when there was timber and fish aplenty, and a good man could tell a boss to get stuffed in the morning and have another job by dinnertime.

I was reminded of this independence the other day, while working on the log booms. The boss and I were on our way to the floating lunch shack for a late lunch when he suddenly veered the boom boat toward the shore.

"Forgot my lunch," Dave hollered over the roar of the engine.

As we came alongside the dock I suggested he hold the boat while I, already on the stern, zoom up and grab his lunch kit.

"No way," he said, looking like I'd just offered to hold

hands. "I'll get my own lunch. Besides," he said, "on this job, there will be no bootlicking."

The remark stung, as similar remarks have stung over the years. There is a code in this kind of work, a rule that says overpolite behaviour equals lack of dignity. The same code says that bootlicking, or grovelling, is for hungry dogs and guys slithering up the corporate ladder. Out on the log booms, where a promotion means you get a longer pike pole, grovelling is as inappropriate as a belch at a fancy restaurant. That is why the boss fetches his own lunch.

Dave doesn't even like to hear an employee say, "I'm working for..." He prefers the more amiable, less servile "I'm helping out..." As in, "I'm helping Dave out on the booms next week." Never mind that he can hire and fire on a whim; he likes to think of work as something done between equals.

Independence is such a given in resource jobs that bosses often insist on it. I used to work in a logging camp where the boss was a short, skinny hardhead who, it was rumoured, fired a man now and then just to keep in practice. The first job Dan, the boss, put me on was chasing on the steel spar. The job consisted of tending the lunch fire and keeping Steller's jays out of the crew's lunches. The first part was easy; the jay part wasn't. I pitched stones at the cocky jays and tried to smoke them away with oil smudges. But the moment I turned my back, they were into someone's canvas lunch bag. In despair, I decided to trap one of the birds, kill it, and display the carcass on a pole. The dead bird would be an example to the rest.

Everything I learned about trapping I learned from cartoons. I emptied my lunch box and propped it, upside down, with a stick. Then I tied a length of string to the stick and uncoiled it over the edge of the road. I baited the trap with a tuna sandwich and tucked out of view. When a jay took the bread, I'd pull the string.

A jay came down and took the bread all right, but the bird was quicker than me and flew off. I rebaited. Next time I pulled the string too soon, the trap fell, and the bird looked at me as if to say, You, my simple friend, should be working. Then it picked up the piece of bread, which had been knocked loose, and flew off.

On I went, wasting food and my boss's money. I was almost out of bread when, from my perch at the side of the road, I heard the crunching of tires on gravel. I peeked. It was Dan. I was shirking the job so clearly, so cleanly, that excuses were not an option.

Dan strode to the edge of the road and stood, thumbs hitched in pockets, staring down at me.

"What's going on?" he asked.

"Trapping birds," I answered, peering past him at yet another jay. "Or at least I would be if you'd get out of the way. Oh, got any sandwiches? I'm out of bait."

It was such a straight shot that Dan didn't know what to do.

"Yeah," he said slowly, "I guess I have. They're in the truck."

He actually started to walk over to fetch his sandwiches, but then he turned and slid down the bank beside me.

"You get them," he said, yanking the string from my hand. "What do you think I am, your slave?"

Moving to the Country

At the end of November I helped a friend and his family move from a Victoria suburb to a nearby area realtors call "the country" and I call "semi-semi-rural." Plenty of trees, room for a flock of chickens, but not enough privacy to walk buck naked with a gun.

Halfway through moving day, Mark, who is normally a sensible person, drove a very large Budget rent-a-truck onto a very soft bit of ground in his new yard. The front tire of the truck mired in mud. As Mark tried to reverse, the truck slid to the right and the mired tire plunged into what we later discovered to be an abandoned septic tank. He called in a tow truck. In attempting to pull the very large moving truck out of the hole, the tow truck driver, who smoked rum-flavoured cigars, broke his tow truck. It started to rain. The tow truck driver swore. Mark said he wanted to fall on the wet grass and curl into a fetal position. In just half a day the pleasant semi-semi-

41

rural property had been transformed into a rum-flavoured, profanity-ridden, despair-wrought wrecking yard. Mark was despondent.

"What a royal cack-up," he said. "You might as well head home."

Head home?

"Not a chance," I said, "this is just getting to the good part."

There is something appealingly chaotic about a move from city to country. It is as if people and machinery sense an ease in the pace and back off a couple turns.

I know I backed off a couple turns when we moved to our cabin. After efficiently loading the truck in Victoria I took the last corner on our driveway too fast and arrived in front of the cabin, sideways, very nearly spilling our belongings like fries onto a plate.

I was once in on a move to the country that lasted three days. It started in Duncan and ended in Groundbirch. My family, who were unhappily running a hotel in Duncan, had decided to return to our rightful occupation, farming. On a solo trip to the Interior my dad had purchased a thousand acres of rolling wheat field and pasture, with a white two-storey house jutting up in the middle. All the place needed was us.

We left Duncan on the last weekend of June: Dad and I in a blue GMC sidestep pickup, Mom in a black and white Dodge and my rotten brothers in an early 1950s beater. It remains the only time in family history that we've had three vehicles running simultaneously.

You learn a lot about people when they move. Adversity of circumstances, like moving or mountain climbing, tests mettle. The first thing I learned on that trip was that my dad wasn't the careful, glad-handing businessman I'd always known. At our family's hotel, all I'd seen him do was gargle and fold towels. As soon as we started up the Fraser Valley, he planted a very large White Owl Invisible cigar in his mouth. For the five years we were on the farm, that cigar never went out. If it stunk, too bad. Farther into the Interior I noticed that my tricycle, in the back of the pickup, was not secured. When we went up a hill the tricycle clanged to the tailgate; when we went down a hill it clanged against the cab. British Columbia is very hilly. As we went up and down, the tricycle took on the role of a metronome, *clang, clang*. I didn't like what was happening to my trike, but I did admire my dad's new-found resolve not to be distracted.

A similar broadening of purpose infected my mom. In Duncan, Mom had been a hard-working dawn-to-dusk type whose favourite saying was "Everything in moderation." Who, then, I wondered from the passenger seat in the pickup, was driving our black and white Dodge when it hurtled past us in a cacophony of cylinders on a double line outside Cache Creek? Mom, it turned out, operated at a different tempo in the country than in town. Drive like a fiend, then pull into a service station and snooze with her head slung back until Dad and I clanged past and tooted her awake.

If people change on a move to the country, machinery changes even more. Just out of Prince George the door handle fell off the Dodge; by Williams Lake the alternator in the normally reliable pickup had troubles; right in the driveway of our new farm my brother's car got stuck.

Our family liked the farm in Groundbirch. Mark will enjoy his new place too, once he gets over the trauma of moving.

"I can't believe I drove onto the lawn," he says. "It's just not like me."

"Of course it's not like you," I say. "You live in a different place; you're a different person."

Weather Lore

Our heaviest winds come from the southeast. They blow up the sound and through the strait, and funnel into our bay. They gain speed as they funnel, so a moderate breeze in the strait will, by the time it reaches our cabin, be powerful enough to take the tops off the balsams.

Our weather predictions, on the other hand, come from the northeast. They blow in from a wrinkly, parbuckled old Englishman who resides about fifteen minutes' hard drive from here. Yorky lives in a highly unauthorized plywood shack, on an absentee landlord's land. We're not sure whether the landlord even knows he's there, or how Yorky makes his living, but we are sure we want him to stay.

Yorky is the local repository for weather lore. He observes, as he says, "things" and deduces forthcoming storms or warm spells. These are handy predictions come haying season. By "things" Yorky means animals, plants, even coffee. Yorky makes his coffee the old way, perked, on a wood stove, with an eggshell added for shine. He once told me over a cup of this coffee that the hot spell we were enjoying was about to come to an end.

"Your corns acting up again?" I asked. Painful corns are about the only weather lore I know, beside "Red sky at night..."

"No," Yorky replied. "Bubbles are in the centre of the coffee today. Good sign. Two weeks ago bubbles were again' the rim. And what have we had? Filthy wet."

Yorky often looks to animals for clues about forthcoming weather. Animals are to weather lore what the satellite map is to the weatherman. Yorky recently told me, for example, that the coming winter will be mild because the Canada geese are flying low. Geese flocking high, he says, cold winter; geese flocking low, mild winter. Or, as he puts it, flocking mild. Last fall Yorky told me that he knew rain was due because clams at a local beach were squirting water more vigorously than usual. I said I'd like to see this for myself, thinking I'd fetch a bucket of clams, but he read my intentions and wisely declined.

To Yorky's credit, it did rain. But that's no big deal. Predicting rain around here in October is like predicting a pig is going to produce manure. It's not a question of if, but how much.

I admire Yorky. I admire a man who lives without authority in a plywood shack. But I'm not so sure about his lore. Like a lot of rural wisdom it seems to me to be based on generalizations of the sort that can't really be proved wrong. Another man, a Swede, once told me in all seriousness that it is a sure sign of rain if dogs roll on the ground, or become lazy and stupid. I beg your pardon. Are not all dogs lazy and stupid and fond of rolling on the ground? With that kind of lore you can't miss. There's always a dog being stupid somewhere, so you're always covered when it rains.

And that's not the only suspect lore I've heard. I've been told fine weather is supposed to turn if a cat sneezes, or wipes its mouth with its feet, or sleeps with its paws over its head, or sits with its back to the fire. We have a cat. Sneezing, wiping, sleeping and sitting with its back to the fire are the only things it does. Maybe we've got cause and effect reversed. If we could only get our cat to stop sneezing it wouldn't rain so much.

I once suggested to Yorky that weather lore seemed suspect—that it sounded good, with references to animal behaviour, but at the core it was hollow. I said it made as much sense to predict animal behaviour by the weather.

"Look, " I said. "Right now there's a light shower outside. So I predict... I predict mainly lazy and stupid dogs, with sneezing cats."

It seemed to me a quick-witted dissection of the whole lore business. Yorky didn't think so.

"You know," he said, stirring yet another cup of shiny black coffee, "from a guy like you, such a dumb idea was entirely predictable."

Magnificent Busts

I work at various jobs for a half dozen people: two men and four women. The men, in their late thirties and early forties, wear checked shirts, caps, and blue jeans held up with hand-punched leather belts that curl like cowlicks. Good men, they nonetheless always look ready to have a rye and a fist fight.

The women are between sixty-five and eighty. They wear seasonal outfits. Spring sweaters, summer skirts, fashionable autumnal jumpsuits. Even in the heat of a late summer afternoon, up to their crusty elbows transplanting bulbs, they are ready to host tea for the Governor General.

Working for men is easy. You show up unshaven, in dirty clothes, and gripe your way through the usual topics: UIC slackers, speeding tickets, beer prices. Working for older women is more complicated. It's as if you are going to help out your dear old mom. Work—the actual shovelling,

47

cutting, whatever it is you're getting paid for—is only part of the job.

Consider what I do for my neighbour Mavis. Mavis lives alone in a big house on a large estate. I always shave before I go to work for Mavis, and dress in clean clothes. She's never said anything to me, but somehow, through her erect posture and quiet demeanor, I feel clean attire is expected. The one time Mavis caught me wearing grubby clothes there was a flash in her eyes, just a glimpse really, that reminded me of the time, long ago, when my mom found a bag of pot in my jeans. The eyes said: "Sixteen years of making good wholesome lunches—and you do this?"

Here's a measure of how I feel when I work for old women: my biggest problem is getting my sweater off on a hot day. The shirt under the sweater rides up, and there is a brief flash of bare back and torso. What to do? I'm thirty-five. I do not feel required to go somewhere private to take off my sweater. But I'm going by 1990s standards. I can't help thinking that Mavis, and the other older women I work for, are living in the 1940s and might be offended by a public baring of male skin. I usually suffer through until tea, then slip the sweater off.

When you work for men, you eat and drink only what you have brought yourself. I have actually sat, thirsty, munching on dry crackers, with a boss who happily guzzled cold juice and popped grapes into his mouth. With an old woman, though, all you bring to tea is yourself. You wash your hands, and, if you're wise, slosh the water over your ears. You sit down. You cross your legs. You lift your pinky, bite carefully at the dry cookies old women always have, enjoy yourself. "Here," Mavis says, "I thought you might like to look at this," and hands me a photo album.

Photo albums are a perk of working for old women. Or they would be, if I weren't allergic to the dust in them. Was dust bigger in the old days, along with cocktails and cars? I'll be looking at a baby picture of their now middle-aged son and "Ab-chew!"

"Here's the old farm."

"Ab-chew!"

"And there's the forest where your cabin is now."

"Ab-chew!"

It wouldn't be so bad if I could just go back outside, but when an old lady hears you sneezing, you get sent home to bed.

Work long enough for an old woman and a couple of neat things happen. First, after a few months, a trim, well-groomed man in his fifties starts to appear in the garden, pointing discreetly to where a tool lies in the bush, or where the splitting wedge is tucked in a corner of the woodshed. He is a mystery at first; then, because you have studied the pictures on the mantlepiece, you recognize him. He's the woman's husband, dead since 1974 but invoked through photos and conversations and reminiscences.

Work longer still—I mean years—and someone else appears beside this man. A woman. A 1940s hair style, a fashionable autumnal jumpsuit. You catch this woman in a movement of the arm, in a sideways look at the fuchsia. And you realize maybe she isn't your dear old mom after all.

One time I was working for a menthol-smoking, heavily lipsticked old woman named June, now dead. During tea we looked at her picture album. Among the crinkly pictures from the 1920s was one of a young woman. She was on a transatlantic steamer, grasping the rails boldly, chest thrust out. She was pretty, and built in such a way I had a hard time not staring.

"Do you know who that is?" June said, coyly.

"No," I said, playing the game.

"That's me!" she said, fingering the edge of the picture. She sighed. "Didn't I have a magnificent bust?"

What to say? I've thought of appropriate things since, but all I could do at the time was sneeze.

Good Junk

I was bashing through a patch of snowberry the other day, looking for the cheap plastic golf balls Lily clobbers, when I stumbled over several large coils of haywire. Six, by my count, overgrown and tracked with slug grease.

This was no small discovery. Haywire is to country people what the Interac card is to serial shoppers: an essential convenience, ideal for poking gunge out of a fuel line or suturing a breached fence.

The haywire was on my landlord's side of the fence. The next time I saw him, I mentioned the find. "There's a half dozen rolls in there," I said.

"No there isn't," Dave replied. "There's seven rolls. You missed one that rolled off to the left. About five feet."

Dave went on to say he had put those rolls there before his daughter was born. She is now sixteen. He's got plans for the wire, he said, but hasn't found the time yet.

There is no such thing as "junk" on this property. The stuff that lies in the bush, and under plywood, cars that sink into the ground and sprout ferns—these aren't junk. They are handy things that are just laid up for a time. Junk, according to my landlord, is a concept for the impatient set. The same set who ship away refrigerators that no longer keep things cold, or kids who no longer obey curfews.

Dave has every refrigerator he ever owned. They stand in a row by his workshop like linebackers, full of welding rods and flower pots. Beside the fridges are Dave's defunct white enamel stoves, and beside the stoves are the remains of his trailer. His life's purchases are good for reuse.

People keep old stuff for any number of reasons. Economy, for instance. Dave sees his fifty acres as a large workshop, laid flat, where he can rummage at leisure for free parts. Like Canadian Tire, without the turnstile. But old stuff also has an impractical value. It makes everything around it look good. Sets it off, the way an ugly birthmark sets off a handsome face. Even the lowliest of shrubs looks good next to a heap of slag.

One September, when I was twenty-six and stupid, some friends and I decided to resurrect a 1961 Pontiac languishing in an old farmer's apple orchard. The Pontiac looked as if earth had come up around it, like a tide rising over a beached wreck. It had been parked a decade before, abandoned to the chickens and then, when the chickens were gone, overwhelmed by blackberries. The tires were flat; the battery was dead. The car, we assumed, was junk.

While the farmer watched from his kitchen window we set to work. In two hours we installed a good battery, inflated the tires and clipped the vines. Then, with the aid of a slosh of gas into the carburetor, the car started. The engine thumped at first, like the mating call of a grouse, then smoothed to a clatter. We clambered in and a friend, in the driver's seat, put the Pontiac in gear.

There was a track around the farmer's farm, and we coursed along carefully, for the Pontiac had no brakes. We laughed at the resurrection. We honked the horn, which made a funny sound. We ran over a water bucket.

When we wheeled into the yard my friend stopped the car by nosing it into one of the apple trees. There was a crunch, and scores of Gravensteins thunked down on the hood and roof. We laughed more, until the farmer hobbled alongside.

"You boys," he said, peering in, "I want every one of those apples picked up. And after that, you put the car back in the bushes, where it belongs."

The Pontiac is still in those bushes, sinking under the million tentacles of blackberry. All it awaits is air in the tires, a jump, and someone who recognizes that junk is a disposable concept.

On the Wild Side

When we first moved to the country, our landlord told us that if we were really, really lucky, we might spot a cougar. In fifty years here Dave has seen just four. Glimpses caught out of a truck window, a furry blur in the woodlot. One cougar he discovered munching on the remains of two lambs. The bullet-holed hide now graces the back of his kitchen chair.

A neighbour of ours has seen more, though she's been at it longer. The Cougar Lady, as she is respectfully known, has shot two, three dozen cougar, and tracked scores more. She is retired now, but at one time her infatuation with the big cats was such that she lugged yards of sand onto game trails throughout the area and raked it flat in order to record, in clear, legible script, the passing of all game, including cougars. By checking the sand traps regularly, the Cougar Lady was able to ascertain when a cat had passed, what it was stalking, where it was headed. All ordered, like messages on an answering machine.

No animal snares the imagination of rural residents like the cougar. The cougar is our great white shark: unpredictable, beautiful, lethal in a way that mocks statistics. One cougar attack has the public resonance of fifty bicycle accidents, a hundred downed pedestrians.

Last week we caught what we supposed was our lucky glimpse of a cougar. Spotting it was as simple as looking out the bathroom window one evening. There it was, on the pond side of the tomatoes, slinking down the fence line between us and the field where Magic, the neighbour's Hereford, and her calf were grazing. I called Lorna and Lily, and we crept out for a better look. Although the cougar had moved to the centre of several bushy firs, we had no trouble locating it. Every other animal—house cat, chickens, rabbits—was staring unblinkingly at the same spot. Their bodies formed a warning semaphore, pointed, as they were, like spokes at a hub.

Moving soundlessly on the lawn, we crept to the top of the garden to get a better look into the firs. The cougar, a young male, was about ten feet long. Four feet of that was tail, which was like a pipe cleaner, held improbably aloft in an *S* shape. The cougar was fixed on the calf. He crouched motionless and taut. Only his feet moved; they padded nervously, back and forth, like a tennis player readying to field a serve.

A nudged rock—something—made a sound. The cougar turned and stared at us. Its eyes were telescopic sights, measuring distance, danger, height—and, it occurred to me, tastiness. We backed away several strides. Amid my retreat, I recalled a Paul Bunyan legend about how, when attacked by a cougar, Paul calmly grasped its tongue and yanked the cat inside out, whereupon it ran off. Would a nearby garden rake, I wondered, be as effective as a legend? Lorna, meanwhile, was recalling something more useful. She had read somewhere that you're supposed to sing to keep cougars from going for your throat. Gently, she started into "Pennies from Heaven."

The mother cow didn't share our caution. Magic's flanks, which I have always thought of in terms of barbecue sauce, suddenly pumped with muscle. Her eyes glared. The cougar made a move, and Magic lunged. *Harrumph*, she snorted—an uncowlike sound—and charged. I was reminded of one of those poster-boy steam locomotives from the 1930s, or maybe John Diefenbaker in full parliamentary flight. Magic the cow had put the chase on the cougar. Along the fence line the two animals ran, sticks snapping, clods and boulders breaking loose. As they disappeared from view we could see the cougar ahead of the cow, its butt and tail bouncing up and down like a dune buggy.

The entire event, we later guessed, took seven minutes. Or was it five? Or fifteen? Wildness like that defies specifics, mocks quantification. Even when I climbed the fence to pace off the cougar's approximate length, I wasn't sure we'd seen the real thing. Not a wonder the Cougar Lady used sand: a paw print is the only thing you can believe.

Three days ago the community cougar hunter came out to check the tracks. His hounds picked up the scent, but it was too faint to follow.

"I guess we were lucky to get such a good look," I said as he loaded up his dogs.

"Not at all," he replied. "I bet there's cougar through your yard every couple weeks. They're watching you all the time."

Part Two

Winter Rains

Country News

Our neighbour's blue pickup wheeled into the yard last Friday, and before Wayne stepped out the door I knew something was on his mind. His eyes bulged like a cow's and he had one of those I-know-something-you-don't grins. The last time I saw that look, Wayne brought news that the church organist had been sacked for playing Abba.

This time Wayne had news of a different sort. He'd just heard that the local cafe—effectively the centre of our universe—was going to discontinue its breakfasts. They weren't making any money off the early-morning crowd of contractors and farmers, and had packed it in. The cafe won't be opening until 10:00 am. "I think they're making a big mistake," Wayne said. "There's a lot of movers and shakers use that place."

For the record, I don't care when the cafe opens. Last fall I tried weaselling a seat at the Table of Truth, where the contractors sit, and failed. I did hang around long enough, however, to notice the movers and shakers didn't move or shake for hours on end, but rather sedately stirred coffee with their forks. I figured I wasn't missing much by having coffee and porridge at home.

The way we get our news in the country is as interesting as the news itself. In the city you get news from newspapers. Their reporters have gone to journalism school and know a hundred ways to hide an agenda. In the country you get your news from a bug-eyed guy in a blue truck, who probably didn't make it past Grade Nine. Like Wayne. His agenda is as clear as the kink in his nose. He has a tractor. He does contract work. He needs the morning coffee shop contacts. When he says the cafe is making a big mistake, we all know he really means he's in trouble.

Sometimes I wish the media hired only Waynes. The news would be refreshingly honest. "I've always hated socialists. After hearing Moe Sihota today, I know why..."

Big news organizations live on bad news. In that way they are like cows: they have to turn everything they ingest into a slimy, acid-ridden cud before it can be properly digested. In the country, depending on who you talk to, any news can be good. The day after I was talking with Wayne, a woman named Patti told me about the cafe abandoning breakfast. Patti sees sunshine and lollipops everywhere, except in gun control legislation. Her take on the cafe was all good. She never did like the sprigs of parsley they served with breakfast, she said, and here was a chance for another restaurant to move in with real breakfasts. Scratch the omelettes and French pancakes, she thought a new joint would do well to offer burgers and Coke for breakfast. Cherry cheesecake, maybe.

Of course, out here everyone knows your agenda. That's what happened when I told Wayne I didn't really care when the cafe opened or closed. "You would say that," he said, snorting and tightening his belt a notch. "You haven't been back since you were blackballed from the Table of Truth."

A Chicken
Never Dies

In early December one of the few remaining chickens from our original flock died. Officially, the cause of Bridget's death was hypoxemia, or lack of oxygen to the brain: her head became separated from her body on the chopping block. In truth, though, Bridget was on the way out anyway. She was eggless, limp of wattle, lacking in the brilliance of eye associated with a vigorous hen. The axe was a mere formality, like the ten-count in a knockout boxing match.

I'll miss Bridget. During the last six months of her life she did nothing but peck listlessly at seed and doze in the coop, one foot retracted into her warm undercarriage. That's the exact sort of behaviour I associate with wisdom and peace.

Bridget was actually the third Bridget of our original flock. The original Bridget was a scabrous ankle-pecker who, after a furious spurt of egg laying, including a one-week stretch of possibly two eggs a day, expired, exhausted by her own biological imperative. I can't say I actually mourned her passing, but Lily, who had named her, did. In my efforts to make sense of death to a wide-eyed five-year-old, I came up with the idea of naming another chicken Bridget. That way Bridget became a concept rather than a thing, and the sense of loss was mitigated.

The idea worked, sort of. The second Bridget—or, as we called her, Bridget the Second—was an extraordinarily average chicken, just the sort of heir, come to think of it, that the British monarchy is in need of: monogamous, productive, slow to seek handouts and quick with a dew worm. Bridget's lone distinguishing characteristic was her left-footedness. Most chickens scratch with the right foot more than they scratch with the left, which is why the left leg of a chicken is more tender than the right. Bridget was the opposite, taking one flick with her right, then two or even three powerful thrusts with her left. Working her deviancy to advantage, she often found feed the other hens had skiffed over.

Unfortunately, Bridget the Second broke her leg playing polo one afternoon and had to be put down. No. That is an exaggeration. Actually she broke her wing, we are not sure how, and took cover far under the coop. Come evening, I left her where she was, gambling the raccoons wouldn't pass by that night. It was a bad bet. The only residual of the short, happy reign of Bridget the Second was a trail of feathers leading to the pond.

So, for the last few weeks, we've been looking for a fourth Bridget. After searching over the ragtags from our original flock, plus a few more hens we have acquired, I was inclined to look elsewhere for a candidate. I thought we might import an aristocrat to be a Bridget, a fluffy stand-alone we could pick up at auction. The rest of my family did not agree. Lorna, in particular, wanted to select a Bridget from our existing flock—

the group she affectionately calls The Girls and I not so affectionately call the The Gang of Eight, because as far as I can see, they are a bunch of right-footed, egg-a-day conformists. Ideal stock for soup, but not leadership.

The issue came to a pitch last week. Lorna and I met in the rain, outside the coop. I was for getting another chicken; Lorna was for designating a nondescript hen from The Gang.

"What's the point of calling *her* Bridget?" I said, trying to distinguish exactly what chicken it was she had selected. "We won't be able to tell her from the others."

Lorna smiled. "You see my point," she said.

Bridget is dead; long live Bridget!

The Happy Valley Line

The Municipality of Metchosin is cleaved roughly east and west by a narrow strip of flatland called Happy Valley. It's a fertile, meandering area renowned for producing early sweet corn and juicy carrots the length of your arm. Happy Valley should be called Unhappy Valley, for all the trouble folks there are having with broken marriages and overflowing septics. Or, as one ex-resident puts it, broken septics and overflowing marriages.

Happy Valley divides the community along economic lines, too. It separates residents on the cheaper rural side of Metchosin, where we live, from residents on the pricey semi-rural side, which is closer to Victoria in miles and in spirit. Woodcutters and egg farmers on one side, wood buyers and herby omelette types on the other.

My friend Ian lives on the Victoria side of Happy Valley. He can afford to because he's vice-principal at a nearby elementary school. He lives in a green and white house on a cul-de-sac named after a one-legged Norwegian pioneer. Both Ian and the house are well groomed, though his clematis is spreading and his hair receding. After school Ian takes his son and daughter ice skating at the rink. When they ride bicycles they wear helmets. He attends all-candidates meetings. He buys the *Vancouver Sun*. By any measure he's a fine citizen, the type aspiring democracies should take cuttings from, and transplant carefully.

I buy the *Sun* too, and consider myself a fair citizen. But when Ian and I get together we sound like newsroom doppel-gängers. We both, for example, started talking tough about national debt at the same time; simultaneously we got pessimistic about the future of the salmon fishery. Those are broad issues, with myriad approaches, yet we happened to arrive at the same position at the same time. Hmmm. Something about that kind of harmony stinks. It's as if we share a brain—one that doesn't belong to either of us.

My friend George doesn't read the *Sun*; he doesn't even get the local paper. George lives on our side of Happy Valley, in a motor home carpeted with hunting magazines. He's skinny, slope-shouldered and untended. A deep furrow runs along the left side of his face, where a chain saw kicked back and bit him. He has other scars too, approximately one for every story he tells. He uses them as verification, the way academics use footnotes. "See," he'll say, unbuttoning his shirt to display a cross-hatched bead of tissue on his shoulder, "that's right where the knife went in." Then, turning to expose a similar scar on his back, "And that's where it came out." I once added George's tales together and came up with the conservative estimate that he's 112 years old.

George lives in a motor home because he moves frequently, sometimes on very short notice. Like when he did a bad thing with the just-legal daughter of a friend, in whose yard George was staying. The friend expressed his anger in such a way that George didn't even have time to coil up the extension cord that siphoned power from the friend's home to George's motor home. George just drove off, dragging the cord, like a runaway horse that's tossed its rider and is dragging the reins. The motor home galloped down the road, with two neighbourhood dogs in chase. The dogs haven't been seen since, though someone spotted a homemade advertisement offering two similar dogs for $10 apiece. The ad was stapled to a telephone pole at the corner of the marina road which, coincidence of coincidences, just happens to be George's latest home.

George, I probably don't need to say, is not your model citizen. He's arrogant. He smells. I wouldn't trust him with my chickens. I see George several times a year, when our paths cross in the woodlot. He runs the skidder. When we stop for coffee, George gives me his own take on the news. For instance, he believes Canada's economic problems have nothing to do with debt and everything to do with communists. Calmnists, he calls them. George claims calmnists are subverting the economy by supplying drugs to the nation's youth. They bring in these drugs via imported footwear. That big "spill" of Nike running shoes from a freighter off the west coast wasn't a spill at all, he says, it was a plan, as organized as a paper route. Wow.

Still, I find George's spin on events refreshing, like the crazy ideas physicists keep coming up with for origins of the universe. No notion is too wacky to try out, no explanation too goofy. He's done for my politics what micro-breweries did for beer drinkers. He's given them variety.

Like Ian and our other friends on the Victoria side of Happy Valley, I believe in hard work. I believe that whoever I work for should make money from my labours. That idea—and it is only an idea—is so firmly embedded I don't even think about it. Unless I'm talking to George. George believes that hard work is ruining the environment. Too many loggers sweating it out to make money for the companies. We were sitting on a log having lunch when he explained this to me. What loggers need to do, he said between spoonfuls of canned chili con carne, is slow down, so companies only make enough money to survive. He paused to suck sauce from his untrimmed moustache. That way the forest lasts longer, and so do the good jobs. He belched, wiped his spoon on some moss, and tossed the can over his shoulder.

I have to admit the appeal of that kind of thinking. But the trouble with hanging around with independents like George is that they don't improve the quality of your thinking. All you can do is listen to them, then repeat what they said. That's what Ian claims, whenever I try recycling one of George's wacky theories on him. "You've been talking to your weird friends again," he says.

He's right, but that's the price we pay for living on the far side of the Happy Valley line.

Scowling at the Woodpile

My woodpiles fall over, I'll confess it up front. As I write I'm looking at a woodpile I made, propped by two two-by-fours, that is still falling. It's going over slowly, as woodpiles are wont to do, but sure as manure stinks, it's going to go. The only question is when—before the winter is out, or after?

The woodpile behind the garage has already fallen over. Last year, one pile went over twice and would have gone three times but I didn't restack. There's a limit to how many times a person should be forced to face his shortcomings.

Woodpiles are the principal weakness in the multilayered skill I'll call wood cutting. I am a competent faller, a good bucker and very good with a splitting axe. But to be good in one category implies lack of proficiency in another. Every animal has to have a butt end, and my butt end is wood stacking.

I once lived next door to a man who did everything well.

When Brent built a compost box, he did it so thoroughly that he never had to think of it again. His yard was perfect in the way a model's face is perfect: beautiful and nondescript. Brent had done so many things so well in his yard that his only remaining task was to lean on the fence that separated our properties and scowl at our unkempt yard. He was good at scowling, too: his brow knitted up like the cable stitch on one of Lorna's sweaters. Brent thought scowling would drive us away, just as his persistence with weed killer had driven the dandelions from his property. "So," he'd say, flicking a speck of lint from his freshly washed green dungarees, "I see you don't remove dandelions until after they've gone to seed. Interesting…" Perfect neighbours, he thought, would have a weed-free tidy yard—just like him. What would he do, I wondered, if he didn't have anyone to criticize?

One autumn I felled three hemlocks that bordered Brent's property. I stacked the wood between two cedars, after carefully laying a sturdy base of planks between them. I took my time stacking the wood, fitting pieces together like a brick-layer. That winter a southeaster knocked the top off one of the cedars, and the top knocked over my woodpile. By strict definition, that woodpile didn't fall over, but the result was that same: I had to repile it. While I was doing this, Brent came by.

"So," he said, slinging an arm over the fence, "I see you pile your wood under the trees. Interesting…"

"I don't mind," I said, fitting another piece into the new stack. "The way I look at it, Brent, if a job's worth doing, it's worth doing two or three times."

No Sensible Child

Last Thursday's snowfall graduated from smattering to storm at about 2:15 a.m. That's when Lorna and I awoke to the crack of a branch, followed by more snaps in rapid succession. A tree was going over. We had gone to bed snickering at a local radio station's attempts to drum a crisis out of what was really a heavy frost; now there was enough snow to take down something that sounded alarmingly big and nearby.

It is a pleasure to see how furiously the mind can work at times of crisis. Normally, I can't imagine far enough ahead to play a good game of checkers. Yet in the moments it took for that snow-laden tree to topple, I climbed out of a dream and took swift mental compass of the forest close by. Aging maple and dying alder to the west, fir snag to the east. The most likely candidate was a gangrenous balsam up the bank. I've seen what a full-sized tree can do to a house: the broken rafters, the limbs that pierce a shake roof like shards. My frenzied speculations had reached the point where I was thinking that Lily's room is nearest the tree's trajectory when I was interrupted by a deadening crash, a shudder, then silence. Wherever the tree had fallen, it had missed the cabin.

In the morning I tramped out in the fresh snow to look for the tree. I am ashamed to say I could not find it. Not up the bank, not by the coop. I suspected the downed tree was in a grove of tall firs near the landlord's place, and Lily and I found it there later. By then my late-night panic seemed a result of my natural flightiness, or of my unfamiliarity with snow, or both.

The nighttime snow completely ruined our day. Which is to say it made our day. Like getting grease on a shirt you don't like—there is good reason to rip the day to rags and don something comfortable. Lorna stayed home from work, Lily didn't go to preschool; I postponed a dozen needless errands. Home was home, rather than a parking spot between jobs, meetings, swimming lessons.

The snow had other compensations, too: I like when there is a real need to do things. From the way the rabbits and chickens were frantically scratching at their compounds, it was obvious food was a must, not a luxury. There was snow to flick from the sagging tarp on the woodpile, the animals' frozen water dishes to thaw and replenish. Wild animals sensed this urgency as well, and a mature eagle soared unusually low over us, its head swivelling from side to side like a bum searching a sidewalk for cigarette butts. All the medium-sized birds were frantic in their pursuit of food, as were the tiny winter wrens. Winter wrens are my current favourite bird. They flit and flick around the chopping block eating subatomic particles of something, ignoring gravity and people in their frenzy. I saw one wren turd on a freshly split bit of kindling. The dropping was so clean and clear that as I looked at it, I thought: mounted on a silver chain, and resting in the cleavage of a pearl-skinned woman, this would be beautiful.

No sensible child will work when it snows, including Lily. The only way I can get her to take on a chore is to talk to her for twice as long as it takes to do the job. If the job has anything to do with stacking wood, then the ratio is three to one. That morning, Lily's task was to rake snow from the chicken run, so the chickens could see their seed. We talked about why it needed to be done, and about what was going to happen if it didn't get done, i.e. no snowball fight. Finally she picked up the rake and started. The snow she was raking looked like waves, she said. Then, pausing to gaze at the untrampled hay field, she said it looked like ripples, or skin on a wrinkly grandparent. With the rake at full stop, the images came on: water, skin, feelings; metaphors heaping on top of one another like drifts. When I interrupted with a reminder that the job was not getting done, she announced her hands were frozen.

"Think of something else," I said, "and you won't feel the cold."

She paused a moment, head tilted, looking to the left, her trademark thinking stance. Then she dropped the rake. "Can't. My mind just pushes the thoughts away," she replied. "Besides, I want to think about the cold."

I can understand that. In our temperate, rainy, sodden, sloppy winters, a rare thing like snow is not to be ignored. It is something to dwell on all the day.

Seasonal Disasters

After ten days of pork crackling, hard European crackers slathered with stinky cheese, and an average of three pickled eggs a day, all I have to say is: Thank goodness for the root balls. They saved the season.

The root balls I'm talking about were attached to the bases of two trees, a short stubby balsam and a tall gangly fir. These two trees grew beside the garage of an elderly neighbour and were loosened in a storm that hit one night just before Christmas. Lily and I spotted them in the morning. They were leaning into the garage at 30 degrees, amid splintered shakes and shattered two-by-fours.

Thus we had our seasonal disaster. Every Christmas needs its disaster—a washed-out road, a ruptured appendix, a runaway chimney fire—something that keeps your mind off all the other things that can go wrong.

I have two lingering fears about late December. One is that

it will be my family's last year together. I fear that somebody will die and Christmas will never again be the same. I've been thinking this way since my friend Kenny and I made each other moribund talking about our families after a road hockey game when we were fourteen. Overweight brothers, aging fathers— we vowed to savour each Christmas as if it were the last.

That was twenty years ago. Nobody in our immediate families has died. Turkey still tastes like turkey, a dog gagging on tinsel still sounds like a dog gagging on tinsel. Twenty years, I think, is too long to savour anything, otherwise I'd still be listening to Peter Frampton. All our Christmases are a pleasant but unremarkable stew of presents, pastries and drowsy afternoons.

All, I should say, except for the Christmases with disasters. How about the Christmas my brother signed himself out of hospital after an appendix operation and gingerly walked to our house? We decided to cheer him up with humour, and very nearly sent him back up to the hospital with torn sutures. That was special. Or this Christmas. I chopped wood from the downed trees on Christmas day, and Lily and I had two big fires and a small fire burning the branches and debris. During one fire a spark went down my back, and Lily got to see me do the cinder jig, the memory of which promises to last longer than any toy, and likely me. We had so much to do and so much fun doing it, we opted out of a party, and I'm doing everything I can to stretch the work for another day.

This leads me to my second seasonal fear. I fear that, come the holidays, there will be *nothing to do*. The nightmare day, which I have endured, is this: an enormous breakfast, then an enormous lunch, then just before an enormous dinner, having to do a 550-piece jigsaw puzzle of a waterfall. The food congealed inside me, like grease on a frying pan. One spark and I would have torched.

With a disaster, however, such concerns disappear. Time

becomes less like gravy and more like water. It passes quickly. The uprooted trees, after they were off the garage and on the ground, were still a hundred yards from my woodpile. The easiest way to transport the wood would have been in my truck. But I was not after the easiest way. I wanted a slow, difficult way: slow to make the job last; difficult so I could work up that rarest seasonal occurrence, an appetite. We used the wheelbarrow. Back and forth. Lily and I worked until we were hungry, then worked for another half hour. By the time we broke for a meal we were so famished we fought for washing space at the sink. Lily sat at one end of the table and I sat at the other, turkey carcass in between. We passed the greasy salt shaker back and forth, eating as if it were our last meal.

The Colour of January

We pay our dues for country living in late January. Grey fog on grey water under a grey sky. There are times I'd happily swap a half cord of dry fir firewood for the brilliant flash of a police light, the lively wail of an ambulance.

Only two colours brighten our monochrome horizon: a valiant orange aconite flower and Leo Steizer. The aconite has popped up by the garage, Leo has popped up by the municipal recycle bins. He was supposed to be gone—and I mean gone—but the doctors hacked out yet another section of tuberous intestine in December. He's had so much gut removed, he says he'll have to chew his food twice, like a cow.

Leo is our resident handyman. Quick with a Robertson screwdriver, swift with a square foot calculation. He is 6'2" tall and wears green worker's pants that come to his chest. The fly on these pants is as long as a tent zipper. Despite his poor health, Leo can hoist two four-by-eight sheets of gyproc and lug them through a living room without knocking over any family photos, which is better than I can do with one sheet of gyproc.

I know this because Leo redid our bathroom walls last fall. While he was here he noticed on our kitchen table a letter with a return address in Smithers. "You got to watch that place," he said, jabbing a big finger at the letter as if it were Smithers itself, and not a flowery letter from our poet/tree planter friend. "Smithers is where it all began."

"All," it turned out, was his stomach. He said his stomach went on the fritz after a lunch in Smithers, in a joint that served chicken chow mein on a cracked plate and Coke in a greasy Pepsi glass. "It's never liked anything tougher than a soft-boiled egg since."

"When was that?" I asked.

Leo thwacked his tape measure several times, thinking. "'61, maybe '62."

That's the thing about guys like Leo. They've been every-where, seen everything. He once watched a construction worker fall from a twelve-storey building, and as the fellow plummeted past each floor he quietly waved to his buddies. Leo put a shake roof on the $300,000 home of an NDP MLA, and the MLA offered to pay cash for a 20-percent discount. The construction worker, he says, had class; the MLA was a fart. "Fart" is a word that appears in many of Leo's political state-ments. That and "turkey." They are spokes in the wheel of his political doctrine, functioning the way "Tory" and "Grit" do for political columnists. He's a curmudgeon, which means he's crabby in a happy sort of way.

While we were working in the bathroom, taping and mixing drywall mud, I asked Leo if he had any ideas on getting rid of stray cats. Other than the one that involves a bullet. We had several strays sniffing around, excavating the flowers—

which, now that I think of it, is why we have only one aconite when we planted a dozen.

"There's only one way," Leo declared, trowelling on mud. "Put the cat in a crab trap and hose it down. Ten minutes. Not five, or seven. Ten. And don't let the yowling bother you, because they'll yowl and their bowels might let go too. But they won't come back." It was so curt, so final, I felt like asking how to turn one buck into a million.

As we worked that afternoon, it occurred to me that Leo has the toughest job in the world. To be cheery and smart, and to know the prices of set screws. I wondered how many people hired Leo to replace a belt on the dryer when they really wanted him to invigorate their days, to class up the high-rise grey weeks with a joke and a quiet wave.

The weather hasn't had any visible effect on Leo, or his green pants. When I saw them at the recycle bins they were both riding high. He had just scrounged a length of copper pipe for a solar project.

"Ever try the cat cure?" he asked.

"Sure did," I said, "worked like a charm."

Truth is, it didn't work at all. We have more strays then ever. But I didn't have the stomach to tell Leo that.

Censored Seeds

I had a couple hours between jobs the other day and decided to pass them in the garden. Except for a few quick dinnertime trips to the parsley patch, no one has even walked by the flower beds since mid-November, maybe longer. I made a big cup of coffee, slipped into gumboots warmed by the woodstove, and stepped outside for some pleasant winter gardening.

The first thing I was going to do was rake the vegetable garden, which was buried in a dandruff of fallen fir cones and needles. But the ground in the vegetable garden was so wet my boots turned the soil to muck. Muck equals compacted ground come planting time. So I thought I'd lime the lawn instead. But the lawn was soft, too; besides, there was no rain forecast for the next week. Lime needs rain. Another day, maybe.

With my rapidly cooling coffee, I walked up to the shack where we have geraniums overwintering, to see how they were doing—if they were marked by rot, or tipped over by rodents.

Censored Seeds

I gave each plant a going-over, slowly turning the chill clay pots in my hands, like a vintner inspecting a glass of wine, and discovered—nothing. The geraniums were fine, which was too bad, because my pleasant two hours in the garden were quickly being reduced to an eight-minute waste of time.

Is there anything more frustrating than gardening in January? We squelch around in the cold, staring at dormant plants, feeling vaguely ripped off by the elements, like a kid with a new toboggan and no snow.

Of course I'm being silly. There are lots of useful things to do in the garden in winter. I have a gardening book that says so. Here's a quote, under a section entitled January Activities: "Sharpen, clean and oil garden tools and clean and service power equipment." I always like a clean rake; they rake so much better. And for cutting through the clay there's nothing like a well-oiled spade. Come on, a tool is a tool, not a Formula One race car.

The same book, one of a dozen remarkably similar, re-markably expensive books on our bookshelf, lists this as an-other January Activity: "Study garden layout and plan changes for next season." Where I come from, studying isn't an activity, it's something you do slouched in a comfy chair, with the heartbeat at a pleasant 45 and a bowl of barbecue chips at hand. As for planning a garden from the depths of winter, I bet the people who write these books buy next year's wrapping paper on Boxing Day.

Compared to seed catalogues, however, gardening books are only modest proponents of winter gardening. Slick and glossy, the full-colour gardening catalogues have been pouring into our house for three weeks now, beckoning us with grandi-ose prose and voluptuous pictures to buy big, buy now.

I've got a problem with the new seed catalogues. They used to advertise like everyone else, with subliminal seduction.

Grow this early rose, they suggested, and your own spore will go far; you too will be coveted. It wasn't true, of course, but at least it was sophisticated. This year, seed catalogues have all the subtlety of a low-budget stag film. Tulips in one brochure are named Debutante and African Queen; poppies are Curlilocks, Harlequin or Turkish Delight. There is a peony called Bowl of Cream, and, for the gardener whose tastes border on the perverse, a rose called Golden Showers.

The descriptions accompanying these names are no less titillating. A tulip named Françoise is described as "a tall, cool, refined beauty"; Madonna is an "exotic spectacle"; Angelique has "huge, peony-like blooms." *Huge, peony-like blooms*? Who wrote this stuff, flunk-outs from the *Hustler* School of Creative Writing?

The description of Angelique, I'll note, is joined to a picture of such lascivious proportions it is curious the censor didn't slap a black bar across the flower's distended pistils. Not a wonder winter gardening is frustrating!

One of the more coyly worded catalogue ads boasts that a miniature narcissus called Tête-à-tête has such perky little flowers that "it's easy to understand why there seems to be a little neighbourly gossip going on." Another suggests teaming a tulip dubbed Queen of the Night with another named Shirley for a "memorable bouquet." "Bouquet" being, I take it, an "in" term, like "Oreo cookie" or "choking the chicken."

I can tell you one thing. Neither the books nor the catalogue are going to work on this gardener. You won't catch me buying from any company that turns seed into sex, and you definitely won't catch me oiling my shovel in January. At least not in public.

Losing Cool

At the back of our garage, tucked in the centre of a rusting metal tool box, rests a broken claw hammer. The hammer head is bright red, hardly ever used, but the handle is broken. My parents gave me that hammer for my eighth birthday. Two days after my birthday, I was working alongside my dad in our farm workshop when he asked to borrow the hammer. He was rebuilding our bulldozer and needed to tap a bearing. Clutching my hammer in his greasy hand, he tapped, lightly at first, then harder, then harder, until there was a click of broken metal. The bearing was bust.

My father's temper is like a quarterhorse. Blisteringly quick off the mark, but not much endurance. He could and did make the transition from rational being to hydrogen-fuelled rocket in a single syllable.

"God-dammit! What the hell's the matter with this thing?!"

And so my new red claw hammer was projected across the

workshop, where it ricocheted off a bench before splintering on a steel girder. Later, when things had cooled down, I fetched the head and put it in the box, where it sits today.

It's one of the great privileges of living in the country to be able to indulge a temper, to howl and bust things. A vigorous temper, I've always thought, is as much a part of a healthy life as howls of laughter. Both are irrational; both are satisfying. I wouldn't be without either.

I once worked in an office where outbursts were not permitted. The men and many of the women who worked in that office had that uniquely sour smell you find in banks, churches and other institutions where expressing emotion is prohibited by law. I now think there was a relation between the constrictions and the smell. Pent-up emotion, which should be released through hollering, formed as a stress-induced stench.

I witnessed just one outburst in that office: a janitor had a fist fight with a photocopier. Both were removed and replaced with quieter, less lifelike models. Their termination was a message for the rest of us not to vault the approved suit-and-tie spectrum of behaviour.

A temper has been such a common trait in our family that it is possible to trace the family history through outbursts. My grandfather had a tantrum the day he backed his new Massey–Harris tractor—the first in the family as well as the district—into an irrigation ditch. My newly married sister blew her top at a fair in Duncan and scorched, by words alone, three drunken loggers and an off-duty fire-fighter. And I had a famous outburst after we moved to Metchosin.

I was trying to cut firewood to heat the house. The saw was very old. My nephew, who had loaned it to me, had said it ran fine. While Lily and Lorna watched from an up-ended cedar burl, I tried to start the saw. I placed it on the ground and pulled; I rested it on the chopping block and pulled; I checked the gas; I pulled again. After what I conservatively estimated was the three-thousandth pull, I let out a short scream and hurled the saw over the bank. Lily and Lorna exchanged tolerant looks. By the time the saw completed its noisy descent through the salal, I was calm again.

The chain saw incident now marks the time we moved into this cabin—another full-colour, sound-enhanced snapshot to add to the family album of upsets and outbursts.

The Horse Lobby

It has been a dismal five days in this part of southern Vancouver Island. Fog rolled off the strait and lay over the farmland like a bad mood. It obscured the sky, the trees, even people's reason. We heard, for example, talk of the horse lobby. The horse lobby is our equivalent of the Masonic cabal, or the Jewish conspiracy. A small but powerful coterie of women with muscular thighs and knee-high black boots are supposed to hold sway over municipal council, bending decisions to their equine agenda.

The horse lobby gets blamed for everything. They force hay prices down and land prices up. They are even being blamed for the spate of door-to-door marketers that are sweeping through the community.

One of these marketers showed up at our house yesterday. A young man in shiny pants. I dismissed him quickly but politely, because I felt sorry for him. He reminded me of my brother Paul, who, during one swampy period of his life, sold handguns door to door for Maclean–Hunter.

"No thanks," I said, "try down the road."

Not all marketers are treated so well. My neighbour Teddy thinks of door-to-door sellers as a scourge, like broom or gorse, to be rooted out and soaked in brine. This week two nicely dressed women tried selling Teddy their version of everlasting life in the hereafter. It was a bad choice on their part, for Teddy has already decided to spend his afterlife in Mazatlán, where he went ten years ago after guessing the number of marbles in a Lions contest. The marbles were in a caulk boot in the front window of Gerry's Chain Saw Shop. Teddy drove home, filled his caulk boot with pea gravel, then emptied the boot and counted the rocks. Two hundred and fifty-eight. He was off by five. He would have guessed right on, he said, but he forgot the wad of tissue stuck in the boot where the big toe should be, since he doesn't have a big toe.

Teddy invited the well-dressed women into his home, a trailer adorned in a suit of cedar siding. He was watching TV. While they talked, Teddy cleaned his fingernails with his pocket knife. When they said something profound, he snorted. They talked and talked until it became obvious than they were going to spend eternity in a cedar-sided trailer, not a place with harps. They slipped quietly out the door, too disillusioned to say goodbye.

"That's how you've got to treat them types," said Teddy, smugly. "They won't be back."

Teddy's brother Daryl didn't fare so well. Daryl lives across the bay, by himself, in a shack with a faded Canadian flag in one window. When Daryl saw an unfamiliar four-door sedan wheel into his yard, he slipped out the back door. He jumped over an irrigation ditch and hiked through the fog to the back pasture, where he's got a portable sawmill. The car followed, splashing through the ditch and into the pasture, then got stuck. A short man got out. He carried a briefcase. For $19 a month, he told Daryl, ignoring the water streaming into his Italian shoes, Daryl could have a life insurance policy that covered everything but earthquakes and cabbage fly. The salesman then played a brave card and said he'd only write up the policy if Daryl got him unstuck. It was such an impressive pitch Daryl couldn't say no.

Yesterday Teddy questioned Daryl about the wisdom of buying a life insurance policy. No wife, no kids. Likely as not the estate would go to the local government.

"And who's that going to do any good?" said Teddy.

The two brothers looked at each other, like they had the same idea at the same time.

"The horse lobby."

Lonely

If there is a dirty lie about urban living, it is that desperate heights (or lows) of loneliness are best achieved in the city. I have been lonely in the city—outside the Commodore Ballroom on Granville Street in Vancouver, to be specific—and I have been lonely in the country. For that unique gut-sickening, headachy pain that is unique to loneliness, nothing equals the country. An empty rural lane, leafless windswept alders, one crow with its feathers ruffled—it's enough to make you think everyone else has departed for another planet and left you caretaker of a used world.

I have been thinking about loneliness lately. Not because I've been without company, but rather because I've had too much company, and wish to be alone. Parties, meetings, family events. I feel like I've been wading in a slush of pleasantries, polite compromises, all the stuff that keeps family and friends coursing along.

I've always thought of loneliness as an irritating buddy, a surly, unshaven cretin with breath like canned cold spaghetti. This cretin peers over your shoulder. He knows what you are really like: that you care more about new jeans than you do about national unity, that you stole a bale of hay from the landlord, that one time when your family was away, you ate only barbecue chips for dinner and thought bad things about the cat. No wonder everyone left for another planet.

The loneliest people I ever met were the Scandinavian farmers who lived in the Peace River country when I was a kid. Many of these farmers were bachelors. They lived in converted granaries, each with one door, two windows and no lawn. During the long winters these bachelors stayed inside their overheated shacks, drank coffee, smoked, and occasionally blew their brains out with a double-barrelled shotgun.

One of the loneliest of these farmers was a craggy, yellow-skinned Norwegian named Russ. Russ had the biggest collection of Amphora tobacco cans you have ever seen. He lived fifteen miles back of the highway, far beyond the reach of electricity or telephones. For entertainment he smoked and played the fiddle. Once a week Russ drove his Chev pickup to the general store, where he stretched a simple purchase of coffee and kidney beans into an afternoon of shopping.

Russ enjoyed an awed community respect for something he did one very long, very lonely winter. It was a cold year, with much snow, and Russ was unable to get to the store. He even missed the great event of the season, the community dance. Nobody saw Russ, and Russ saw nobody. Come February he was so lonely his teeth hurt.

There were mice in Russ's shack. To fracture the awful silence that winter, he trapped the mice. He put them in a pot and placed the pot on the woodstove. While the mice squeaked in agony, Russ fiddled in concert. After Chinook winds melted the snow and the roads reopened, Russ told people he wasn't proud of what he'd done, but he was proud to have made it through the winter. The company of the mice helped preserve his sanity.

Dad and I used to visit Russ. The dirt road home from the river led by Russ's place, so we would stop in after fishing. Russ was always friendly, ready with a pot of something he called coffee. His cookies were stale, his tarpaper shack too warm, his conversations halting. Russ's conversations never got going, just as some people's conversations never stop.

Once, after forty-five minutes of surging stop-and-go talk with Russ, Dad said it was time for us to head home. We stood up.

"Don't go," said Russ. It was an uncharacteristic blurt. He licked his chapped lips and studied us with eyes too weather-worn to tear.

"Don't go," he repeated, softly. "Not yet. Stay. We don't have to talk about anything." He said the last word "anyting." It was honesty of a sort I've heard a half dozen times in my life, a palpable declaration to be pocketed and rubbed smooth with your fingers.

"Don't go. Stay."

We stayed with Russ until the shadows of the trembling aspen darkened his shack. We left him leaning in his doorway, fingering another homemade cigarette.

I said loneliness is a companion. To endure it every day, as Russ did, would be too much for me; never to endure it at all would be to miss a wise and surly friend.

The Kids Will Be All Right

There weeks ago my landlord and his wife flew to the South Pacific, leaving the farm in the care of their teenagers, Walt and Sonja. The morning after they left, the driver's side door vanished from the family hay truck and Magic broke through the fence and escaped down the driveway. Lorna was concerned, and suggested we help, but I said no; this is what is supposed to happen when parents leave kids in charge. I was working on my old truck at the time, and by way of metaphor squirted some liquid hand cleaner in Lorna's direction. I said teenagers too had a way of loosening and unfastening everything around them. Part of the growing process.

I empathize with teenagers. Not only because I still fiddle with trucks and borrow money from my parents, but because when you're in your thirties, as I am, the logic of teens is still fresh. I understand why, for example, my brother drove Dad's bulldozer across the lawn when the folks were holidaying in

Osoyoos. Guy, age seventeen at the time, was trying to push over the outhouse, and thought the lawn easier on the 'dozer tracks than beating through the bush.

In the same way, I understand how my friend John came to ruin his father's Chev station wagon. John's parents had left on a freighter cruise of the South China Sea, leaving John to tend their small farm. Soon after the parents left, John began arriving at school in the family tractor. Sometimes he pulled a small trailer. One day he loaded the trailer with females from his Biology 11 class and carted them to a fashionable restaurant. A teacher saw them and told John that carrying students in a farm wagon was a stupid, irresponsible thing to do. John agreed, went home, transferred everyone to the family station wagon and took them to a better restaurant in Lake Cowichan. On the way back from Lake Cowichan they spotted an enormous sawdust pile, with long tapering slopes, beside the highway. They discovered a road leading to the top of the pile, and after a quick democratic vote, they drove off the edge of the pile. Around and around the perimeter of the pile they spun. It was so entertaining that for three weeks sawdust piling, as it was known, was made part of the curriculum, along with sleeping in Social Studies and pouring urine samples into the biology teacher's rare-fish aquarium.

John's parents were elated on their return to find the family estate in good shape. But the next week, his father, who is a lawyer, was travelling to some important lawyer thing when the wagon caught fire. The smoke, he said, smelled like wood. The mechanic who did the $1500 rebuild claimed he hadn't seen so many wood chips in an engine in twenty years of monkeywrenching. Said it was a credit to the House of Chev that the engine survived as long as it did.

All this was going through my mind as I watched the landlord's kids over the last few weeks. First there was the truck door, then the fence. Then there were weird tracks through the hay field, and some late-night crashing and banging in the shop. One morning, a school day, I saw Walt and three youths out in the family's aluminum skiff. I began planning to take a little holiday when the parents come home, to avoid the fireworks.

Yesterday I met Walt at the mailbox. He was in the hay truck.

"Any other doors fall off?" I asked.

"Fall off?" he said. "I took that door off. Dad's been having trouble with it for months. Worked all day to get it back on. Ground the valves on the engine, too."

"Oh," I said, suddenly ashamed. "What about the tracks in the field?"

"Cutting wood. Never too early to lay in firewood."

Mmmm. I thought about the boat. You can't explain a boatload of kids skipping class.

Walt could. Biology project, something to do with intertidal life.

"Sounds like things are fine," I admitted.

"You know," Walt said, "when you get right down to it, things run a lot easier when the folks aren't around."

Then, with the gentlest of clicks, he shut the door.

Part Three

Seed Time

Real Farmers

Alice, the cow who lives up the road, is an 1100-pound red and white Hereford. Every spring Alice calves under a cedar windfall in the northwest corner of the field. Every spring Gord, the farmer who owns her, calls the calf Hope. This cycle has been going on for four or five years with the current Alice, and it went on for twice that long with earlier editions of Alice. The reason there aren't a dozen or more Hopes around is that every fall Gord sells the previous year's Hope for cash. Or he has Hope butchered, returned in brown paper packages marked Plate Brisket, Foreshank and Rump in black felt pen, and stacked in one of the two long Kenmore freezers he keeps in his basement.

Gord is a real farmer. By that I mean he makes money off his farm—or at least tries to—instead of pouring money into it, as so many pretend farmers around here do. A pretend farmer wouldn't call a calf Hope. He'd call it Edison, or Hobbes, or, if he was literary, Ishmael.

The Ideal Dog and Other Delusions

The names they choose for their livestock are just one way to tell the difference between pretend farmers and real farmers. Another way is to drop in to the local cafe. If it's a Saturday, you'll see lots of $300 cowboy boots and Caesar salads. They belong to the pretend farmers. Real farmers go to the cafe every day *but* Saturday, and they wear black Romeos and eat greasy combo hamburgers with double fries and salty gravy on the side. Pretend farmers predict rain on the hay by squinting at the sky and consulting a barometer; real farmers phone Weather Canada's haying hot line, the number for which they have programmed into the memory of their cellular phones. Pretend farmers stroll around their acreage; real farmers drive fifty feet from the barn to the house. Pretend farmers say "dung" or "cow patty." Real farmers never say "dung" or "cow patty."

The critical difference between real farmers and pretend farmers is in their attitude toward killing livestock. For the real farmer, like Gord, the slaughter of a cow or a pig or several chickens is cause for celebration. Not only is he one step closer to getting much-needed cash in hand or valuable meat in the freezer, but he is also saying adios to an animal that's probably been kicking, butting, pecking, tromping over his feet or dumping on the seat of his tractor for the last three years.

For the pretend farmer, on the other hand, the death of a barnyard animal is a nasty and sometimes unexpected end to an otherwise peaceful human–animal relationship. Several years ago I was renting a room off a young logger named Mike who, in the course of drinking beer and thumbing through *Harrowsmith* one afternoon while he was laid off for fire season, decided that farming his small rural plot might be a pleasant way to spend the summer.

Mike's friend Sean, a seasoned farmhand, convinced Mike he should go into chickens. Chickens, Sean explained at the kitchen table, were the easiest of farm animals. All that's required is a raccoon-proof shelter, a heat lamp and some feed. In six weeks they go from zero weight to four pounds each, whereupon they are butchered, cleaned and sold for several dollars each. Little care, little maintenance, no $150,000 tractors, and the first agricultural profit is in hand.

The chicks arrived from Buckerfield's in cardboard boxes. But from the moment Mike and Sean tipped them into the coop—an old Bowler trailer that had died amid the weeds—it was clear they had differing views of farming. Where Sean saw poultry product, Mike saw 150 peeping, cheeping, squeaking puffs of yellow dandelion. Even after several weeks, when the cute chicks had grown to become stinking, awkward, squawking teenage chickens, Mike still enjoyed tending them. He fed and watered them in the morning, and in the afternoon he'd take a beer and shuffle around saying hi to his favourites. Sean, when he did show up, goose-stepped in and out of the flock.

One of Mike's pets was an unusually orangey-red chick that was first out of the coop in the morning and last one in at night. It was the only chicken with the smarts to escape, which it did twice—once through a hole under the coop, once between Gord's legs as he slipped through the door in the wire compound. "That chicken could have been prime minister if it wanted," Mike would say, looking at it fondly. "Of course, it's too smart for that."

Six weeks rolled around, then seven. The dandelions turned into porkers. Sean wanted to butcher the lot before they got fatty, but Mike always found some excuse why it wasn't convenient. Eventually though, fire season ended and logging resumed. One day while Mike was at work, Sean bundled the chickens into burlap sacks and carted them off for slaughter.

Next evening, Sean came around with Mike's share of the profit. But Mike wasn't interested in money. "Did you have to kill *every* chicken?" he asked, gazing at the lifeless trailer.

Sean followed his eyes. "Geez, I'm sorry about that, Mike," he said, touching a hand to his hat. "If I'd known you wanted to get in on the butchering that bad I would have waited..." He was going to say more, but stopped. Like all real farmers, he was good at saving himself from grief.

Accounting for the Woodpile

When a surprise southwest gale recently toppled three tall balsams on an adjoining property, I was invited to salvage the wood. The drawback was that the trees had gone over in an area I couldn't get my truck into. After cutting the logs into rounds, I had to wheelbarrow them up a path to the driveway, where I halved and quartered them. I tossed the chunks in my truck and drove my truck to our yard. Then I carried the pieces from my truck to the woodpile, where I stacked them in sturdy, rectangular rows. By the time I was finished I had touched every piece of wood a half dozen times, and knew each so intimately I could have named them.

The stack measures out to 650 cubic feet, or slightly more than five cords. Purchased from a wood seller, five cords bought at this time of year would cost $500. And $500 divided by the several days it took me to cut and haul the wood, to say nothing of the cost of gas and oil for the chain saw or the stainless steel thermos I squashed, works out to about $5 per hour. It is clear from the bookkeeping that if I work hard and long at this sort of money-saving venture, I'm destined to go dead broke.

That is the sort of accounting dilemma we regularly face in the country. Do you justify the time it takes to put up your own wood, and grow food in the garden, and put up preserves, by traditional economics? Or do you ignore accounting altogether, pick blackberries until you are purple, then have to beg off another month's rent? The former is retentive banker's thinking, the latter plain irresponsible.

One answer, suggested to me by a moustachioed, cleft-chinned friend named Eric, is that we need another form of accounting, as rigorous as an actuarial table but incorporating elements other than interest rates. For instance, Eric would include in his accounting a heading titled Appetite. Eric is a lawyer. Most of his days are passed at a desk. His tiny appetite is a function of the office clock, not his body. When he works on his small farm, however, he generates a large appetite. He says he pays $1,000 a month mortgage for the hunger, and the farm gets thrown in for free. He tallies his meals at $12 each.

Also on Eric's accounting list: Pleasurable Weariness and Sound Sleep. The ecstasy of a sore back and swollen forearms is not something you can buy. After a day digging fence post holes in his heavy clay soil, Eric goes directly from work clothes to bath, and bath to dressing gown. He lies on the floor in front of the fire and emits a low, self-satisfied groan that lasts for three hours. The post holes he could have had dug for $2 each; the evenings he figures are worth $50 apiece.

Perhaps the most profitable feature of Eric's accounting system shows up under the heading Interesting & Innovative Thoughts. With the body occupied in shovelling manure or other physical activities, his mind is free to holiday. It goes where it wants, riding notions bareback. Work. Family. The corner of the pole barn that is sloughing into the creek. Such freedom isn't cheap, Eric said to me one day, so he bills out at $200 a day. And you don't need many $200 days, he declared, to change the gloomy economics of farm projects.

It took Eric the best part of a morning to tell me about his accounting system. He was on one side of his fence, leaning on his shovel the way Charlie Chaplin used to lean on his cane, and I was perched on my truck. Finally I said I had to go.

"We're not making any money standing here," I pointed out.

Eric shook his head. "You don't understand," he said. "The way I've got it figured, we're making lots of money shooting the breeze. It's work we can't afford to go back to."

Befriending Kids

Last week I devoted myself to befriending a four-year-old girl. Connie attends preschool with Lily. She's the youngest child of a horsey couple down the road. Green-eyed and freckled, she's smart enough to stay away from the back end of a cow, yet innocent enough to consider raw broccoli a treat. An ideal playmate for Lily.

We invited Connie to come to our house, but she was shy, especially of swarthy men with nose hairs. She would not agree to ride in our truck, let alone stay with Lily and me for an afternoon. My task, Connie's mother and I decided, was to make the girl comfortable, to let her know I was OK.

The trouble with university education is that it disinclines you to think for yourself. Confronted with a simple problem, like befriending a child, my instinct is to reach for a book or consult an authority. The authority I reached for this time was the memory of an old family friend. Uncle Ernie—as he was universally known, even to his wife Rose—was the most popular person with kids I've ever seen, which was strange since he had long nose hairs, too. They sprung out of a bent leathery nose in a leathery face that, before he quit drinking, was usually plastered to the bar of the Tzouhalem Hotel.

Ernie had many tricks for making kids feel at home. When you went into his house he didn't say hi or even turn around. He kept on picking at his African violets. That is all Uncle Ernie did. To a kid, used to seeing adults make happy faces and pretend to be oh-so-glad to see you, Ernie's unaffected candour was as refreshing as a cold root beer.

I was thinking of Ernie when I picked up Lily from preschool on Monday. After school is usually a time for parents to play with the kids, who are outside. But what I did on Monday was nothing. I didn't look at anyone, especially Connie. Didn't say a word.

Such an approach may have worked for Uncle Ernie, but it didn't work for me. Nothing happened. In fact, the less I did, the more the kids stayed away from me. Connie, I noted, remained on the exact opposite side of the yard. I could very nearly see her thinking: "If other kids stay away from that guy, I will too."

On Wednesday I changed my ploy. Occasionally, if a child at Ernie's place was looking forlorn or left out, Ernie would step quietly behind him, clasp his ankles with his liver-marked hands and hoist him upside down. Coins, bits of string and pine cones tumbled from the kid's pockets past his head. While he screamed in surprised joy, Ernie laughed. Sometimes, if your pants were loose, you'd squirt out like a wiener from a bun and crumple onto the floor. It was so much fun, in a traumatic way, that you'd see kids intentionally looking forlorn, in the hopes Ernie would tip them upside down too.

When I arrived on Wednesday, Lily and Connie were

sharing a tire swing. "We want a push," they said. Thinking of good-hearted Ernie, I laughed and gave them an energetic underduck. Up, up, up, until the ropes went slack and the beam of the swing bent with their weight. If it wasn't traumatic, it was a first cousin. "Stop!" they both hollered. White-faced, they got off and wobbled to the sandbox.

Last Friday was my duty day at the preschool. A duty day is when you stay and get in the way of the instructors, instead of clearing out. One of my jobs was to read a storybook. I perched on a small chair and the kids fanned out on the floor, like fish holding in a stream. The book was *Snow White and the Seven Dwarfs*. I have not read *Snow White* since I was a kid. It is a horrible book. Seven weirdos in the mountains, poison apples, and at the end the Queenie dances in red-hot metal shoes until she dies? No wonder kids are shy of adults.

I read, slowly, glancing at all the kids but Connie. Through the poison apple part, past the prince part, to the part where the queen goes to the ball. Just then, a very small foot, belonging not to my daughter but to Connie, eased ahead and, with impossible softness, came to rest against my sock.

Uncle Ernie would have been proud.

The Five-Dollar Barn Cat

In strictly economic terms, the worst decision I ever made was buying a barn cat for $5. We got her to kill rats. We brought her home in an apple box and named her Luba. The first afternoon we let her out, she killed a red squirrel. The next day she killed another squirrel and another. Within one week of getting Luba, our lawn was littered with squirrel tails and those funny little stomach bags that must contain something distasteful to a cat. But no dead rats.

We provided cat food, on the welfare-state concept that it was a backup to her rodent intake. Luba took to sleeping alongside her dish, so her mouth could have a few crunches without disturbing her slumbering body.

I reset the rat traps. Luba stepped in a trap. We incurred an $80 vet bill. While Luba was repairing, she got pregnant. She had nine kittens. One of these kittens made a mess on the floor. I cleaned the mess, but failed to wash my hands properly.

I got sick. I had to go to the hospital. While I was in the hospital I missed three days of $200-a-day logging work.

One morning soon after I got out of hospital, I noticed an S-turn in Luba's tail. At that time Lily was experimenting with slamming the sliding glass door. I jumped to the not unreasonable conclusion that she had squished the cat's tail in the door. I gave her hell. I took Luba to the vet. The vet said the injury was actually a bite and could in no way have been caused by a sliding glass door. Then she gave me a bill for $150. Exactly eight months after purchase, the five-dollar barn cat had cost us $830 and my daughter's confidence, and we had just as many rats. I would have been better off posting a $50-per-head rodent bounty.

Cats are like great literature. They are boring and have no obvious value. They are difficult to understand. This is the opposite of dogs, who are interesting and easy to figure out. A dog's philosophy is simple. If a dog cannot eat something or have sex with it, he or she will urinate on it. A cat, on the other hand is—no pun intended—a professional fence-sitter. I have passed whole evenings trying to fathom Luba, and I still don't understand her, just as I do not understand *Finnegan's Wake*. After three years with Luba, I'm not even sure she likes me. When she wants out of the cabin, which is about once a month, she perches on a table with her back to me. When she wants food she sits atop the TV with her tail hanging over the screen, so we feel like we're watching through a furry windshield wiper. Like all cats, she knows many expressions for irritation and only one for happiness, and that is digging her claws into your collarbone.

Sometimes I think the problem is that cats are not cut out for life in the country. I read that a cat can survive a fall from an eleventh-storey balcony. This is not proof of their toughness so much as it is proof that they have adapted to city life. No pig could survive a tumble like that. Of course a pig wouldn't be snoozing on an eleventh-storey balcony.

When Luba had her kittens, we allowed Lily to keep one. She chose a slow-witted hairball whom we dubbed Rolly. For six months Rolly did nothing and grew enormous. One of the few times he ventured out he had his stomach ripped open by a large animal and we incurred yet another vet bill. He convalesced, then tried mating with his mother, then left. That was a month ago. We don't think he's coming back.

Talk about trouble. Lily is worried about Rolly, Lorna is worried about Lily, and I'm worried we might have to buy another five-dollar barn cat. The only creatures in the house who aren't worried about our cat problems are the rats.

Higher Education

I have two things that irritate the neighbours. A moldy brown Chevette that doesn't run, and a university degree. The Chevette, up in the woods, I justify as a backup chicken coop; the degree, in my bottom dresser drawer, is more complicated.

"What can you use it for?" my neighbour Wayne asked a while back. It's one of those sneaky simple questions which, once you've been to university, you are incapable of answering. Like my other neighbours, who were educated at the school of hard knocks, Wayne seems to feel that my degree is an encumbrance of sorts, like a gimpy leg or an extra incisor, and that I'd feel better if it could be put to use.

My response these days is to repeat something someone famous said. (That's one thing a degree is good for, by the way: learned quotes.) In this case the person is Stephen Leacock. A degree, Leacock said, wasn't *good* for anything. Rather, it's a formal declaration that the recipient is full, and cannot learn anything else. That seemed to satisfy Wayne for the moment.

Years ago, when I was migrating between university in the winter and a sawmill in the summer, I used to take exception to questions about my studies. I remember Ted, the loader operator at a sawmill, harassing me in the lunch room: "History, what good's that going to do you?" he guffawed. He was tall and thin and had a long face, like a horse.

I had more gumption then, and I replied by way of my own question. "What's the use of moving all these logs around?" I said. "They're only going to be turned into pulp for newspapers."

That was a mistake. Ted liked newspapers, especially ones featuring Sunshine Girls. Next day Ted drove the loader over my favourite chip shovel.

By the time I graduated from university I had a different approach to questions about higher education. The public had helped finance my education, I said to myself, and I was ethically bound to give them an explanation of its many benefits. I was logging upcoast in a swampy valley off Phillips Arm. It was October, and filthy wet. The hooktender I was working with asked what I was going to do with my degree. It was the chance I was waiting for. "Cliff," I said, wringing out my gloves, "I'm not going to *do* anything with the degree." I launched into a mixed-up thing about the satisfaction of studying Jean-Paul Sartre and existentialism and how there was no meaning to anything and all that. On I went, until Cliff's eyes actually rolled. They became blank, like a late-night TV screen. Clearly Cliff had abandoned Sartre and me to go salmon fishing. Then I realized the problem: you can't tell a logger, standing in the rain on a log-strewn swamp, about things like existentialism. They are doing it.

For that matter, you can't tell a country guy about Stephen

Leacock. A week after I had quoted Leacock to Wayne, Wayne confronted me at the mailbox.

"I think what you told me was a bunch of shit," he said. "I was talking to Steve Leacock himself down at the feed store and he says he never had a degree—and he doesn't want one either."

My Brief Career as an Editor

Whenever we're too poor to afford good coffee, or I feel I'm wasting my time trying to eke out a living in the country, I wonder if I shouldn't get a "real" job. "Real" meaning a city job, with a computer and yellow stickums and a salary.

One of those jobs came up the other day. It was in the newspaper. Wanted, it said, editor for a gardening magazine. Lorna was rolling coins at the time, a sure sign I should apply. A phone call later and I had a job interview.

The interview was on a Tuesday morning. I had a businesslike coffee and cigarette, and, remembering the words of my Grade Ten counsellor, I cleaned and hygiened. I hauled out my only formal jacket, an old tan corduroy, and a black turtleneck sweater. Lorna said I looked like a 1960s spy. I said don't laugh, I look like a regular paycheque. Then I grabbed my briefcase, gave her a businesslike peck on the cheek, and left.

My interview was in the Saanich Peninsula, at my prospective boss's house. As soon as the door opened, I knew everything was going to be fine. Mr. Arnold, as he introduced himself, clearly thought like me. If I was a 1960s spy, he was a 1960s dinner party. He was a walking advertisement for the synthetic textiles industry. He wore a wide tie, a lovely cream cardigan, and that type of pants my mom calls "slacks." His lone concession to post-1965 style was a pair of black, shiny, high, zip-up Beatle boots.

Mr. Arnold ushered me into a white office with no plants. The walls were lined, I noticed, with books on making money. "So," he said, "you're looking for a job?"

I hate that type of question. The seventeen-year-old in me always wants to say something snarky, like: "No, Mr. Arnold. Actually I represent a wealthy international client who wants those boots. Name your price."

But I remembered the rolled coins and succumbed to reasonableness. I told him I'd worked for several newspapers and magazines and had a budding, if not blooming, career. Something was wrong, though. In part it was the look on Arnold's face, which suggested naked Caribbean daydream; in part it was a stabbing pain in my lower back. One of the safety pins holding in the lining of my ancient jacket had come undone, and was protruding at an angle.

"Oh!" I said.

"Is there something the matter?" asked Arnold, irritated.

"No, no," I told him. "I just remembered something else: I won second place for a haiku in junior high. I can write poetry too."

Arnold looked at his wristwatch. "OK," he said, "we don't have much time. So what have you got for me?"

"I beg your pardon?" I said.

He pointed at my briefcase. "What have you got for me? You know, samples of your writing."

Now this was something the Grade Ten job counsellors hadn't prepared me for. There was supposed to be something *in* the briefcase.

"Right," I said, "a sample of my writing." I hoisted the briefcase, flicked it open—and wow, was that banana ever ripe. It had become as one with a freebie guide to trout fishing lakes of southern Vancouver Island. Regrouping, I quickly produced the guide and said it might be a model for the gardening publication. Attractive layout, short concise editorial, lots of room for money-making ads. The idea, if I had one, was to start talking about fishing, and by that means avoid the awkward consequences of being unprepared for the job interview.

The ruse didn't work. Arnold didn't like fishing, and he hated wasting time. "I think the interview is over," he said. "You'll be hearing from me." He guided me right out of the house to the patio and beyond. Clearly he knew of my dormant, snarky seventeen-year-old, and wanted no mad lunges at his boots.

Today I received a letter from Arnold. I got as far as "Dear Applicant" and scrunched it up. But I don't care. Just this morning I got a call from a neighbour who needs new ground broken for a garden. That will take care of this week's grocery bill. And after that? Maybe Arnold needs a tan corduroy jacket.

A Veteran Greenhorn

Our household finances perch on the rickety legs of several part-time jobs. Wood cutting, knitting, and something I call garden labouring, which is really the grab bag of tasks required to keep a rural yard functioning. This week I'm digging a ditch. The ditch is a late addition to a new garden created by our neighbour Frank. It's a late addition because Frank recently discovered, after her underground sprinklers had been installed, that her garden is a quagmire. When it rains, or when Frank irrigates, the soil becomes porridge. My job was to dig a ditch, lay drainpipe, and backfill with drain rock.

"Watch out for the sprinkler pipes," said Frank. The pipes are pricey. Ten minutes into the job, I swung a mattock clean through a small white pipe. I cursed my carelessness, and carried on. An hour later I did it again. By lunch I had excavated just thirty feet of trench, but had busted two pipes.

A Veteran Greenhorn

"Oh well," said Frank, with a long-suffering sigh, "it can't be helped."

Of course it could be helped. I felt like a liability, and was put in mind of a time on the farm where I grew up, when I was learning to drive tractor and skewered the barn doors with the manure forks. "It couldn't be helped," said Dad.

That's the thing about being a generalist: you are by definition a professional greenhorn, the perpetual thirteen-year-old, always making mistakes, always atoning for them.

When I was twenty-three, I took a job installing sewer pipe. My job was to rake the trench clean, then, using a brush slathered with a very potent single-malt glue, stick the lengths of pipe together. My boss, a squat Greek Canadian named Jerry, supervised my work between trips to his office, by which he meant the local bar. "It's the office work that's killing small business in this country," he'd declare. I suggested he come down in the fume-laden trench, where intoxication was cheaper.

One day, after an especially long session at the office, Jerry returned to check my work. "The pipe," he hiccuped, "it's all wrong." I was supposed to be gluing male fitting to female, but had been gluing female to male.

Jerry slumped onto a pile of gravel. I was so embarrassed I offered to stay late and redo the work on my own time. But my boss shook his head. No, he said, that wouldn't be professional. Only professionals on his crew. I passed the rest of the summer indentured to Jerry, like a feudal serf.

Most people gain proficiency at a job through repetition. The trouble with seasonal labouring, though, is that often a whole year passes between those repetitions. This is what happened the last two years on the farm where I hay. For several weeks each spring I drive a small Ford tractor, cutting, turning or baling. After the hay is in, I don't drive a tractor until

117

the following spring. Last year, when I was cutting hay on a particularly thick section of a low-lying field, the mower became clogged. I stopped the machinery, cleaned the mower and restarted, only to have the same thing happen again. The farmer, who was working in a nearby field, came over to help. After the third time the mower clogged, I apologized.

"Don't worry," he said, "it can't be helped."

I contritely said he'd probably get as much done by himself, and save the wages.

"Maybe," he said, "but it's not until you come around that I realize just how much I know."

The Law of Compensation

There are few things I believe in religiously. Three of them are children, cheese and, most of the time, a thing called the Law of Compensation. The Law of Compensation states that misery must of necessity follow joy, and vice versa. This explains why, after last week's span of earth-warming, bud-inducing sunshine, we are socked in a foggy chill that the wood stove is hard pressed to fend off. This explains why, after a vigorous morning of rock picking yesterday, I am now laid up, with a bag of frozen peas pressed against my back.

Nowhere is the Law of Compensation more evident than in the lives of those who work outside, at hard manual jobs. Old-timers around here, in lucid moments, like to say they shaped the land. They felled the trees and carted away the topsoil. But the truth is the land has shaped them, too. What about Jack Gibson, the oldest working beachcomber on the coast, whose hands are so swollen from immersion in icy waters that he can no longer roll a cigarette or splice an eye? Or a man I only know as Emil, with the squashed nose and arthritic shoulder, who needs a younger man to fuel and oil his chain saw, then start it for him? Their damaged and worn bodies are evidence of a natural reciprocity.

I once worked with a guy who shed an alarming amount of his body over the course of five years. His name was Fred, but we called him Parts, because he was always losing them. This was in a shake and shingle mill in Cowichan. Shake mills are notorious for lopping off digits, and there was never a time at the mill when five men could have held up fifty fingers. Floppy-fingered gloves were part of the attire, like the straining gut buttons on a salesman's shirt.

Parts hired on as an able-bodied man. The only thing he was missing, besides Grade Eight and up, was one little toe. He said it had been removed after he dropped an anvil on it. How you drop an anvil on only your little toe was a mystery to me. But then, this was the same guy who successfully robbed a bank in Courtenay, only to be nabbed in a nearby bar counting out fifties and hundreds on the table. For this dim-wittedness he had done two years in jail and was facing several more on probation.

Parts's first job at the mill was working the cut-off saw. The cut-off saw snicked two-foot blocks off cedar logs. One day Parts simultaneously left his foot under a hydraulic ram and pressed the lever that moved the ram. His scream was heard a mile away. Miraculously, his foot was only bruised, but a toe had to be removed. After that he was put on a cuber machine. A cuber machine splits shakes from a block. It is simple and fairly safe. Parts left a hand sitting atop the block, instead of the side where it should have been, and nicely snipped off the tip of his index finger.

And so it went, with Parts working at the mill, and the mill working on Parts. He lost a thumb in a band saw, got a board in the crotch and a log on the head. The last two he said did no lasting damage, and we had no inclination to test his claim.

Parts's stay at the mill came to an end one spring day, when he announced he was quitting. It also happened to be his last day of probation. He'd paid his dues, he said. He knew better ways of making a buck. The last we saw of Parts was when he walked out of the mill yard. He turned and gave us a quick wave, on a hand with 4.3 fingers.

To the rest of us, stuck at the mill to pay mortgages, or scrimping for university, his nonchalance seemed grossly unfair, a fluke of unnatural justice. He was free and we were not. Yet another example of the Law of Compensation.

Humane Traps

For three and a half years we have been uneasy neighbours with a family of raccoons. We liked them, and they liked our eggs. Occasionally, they liked a chicken. As long as the killings were infrequent, we tolerated their presence. We thought of a hen's death as the manifestation of a larger natural equation, and we used the loss to discuss the cycles of life with Lily.

Last Thursday, however, the relationship with the raccoons turned. That's when I discovered the remains of our last mature hen. Actually, I discovered her beak. That's all the raccoons left of Pinky, in an exploded mess of feather, near the coop. Pinky's death followed a bloody two-week spree in which we lost five other mature hens. The killing of this last bird, a peaceful, wise, self-reliant hen who never soiled her eggs, was an unforgivable affront. Like a gob in the eye when you've been kicked low.

Our instincts—and I use that word carefully—were to

shoot the raccoon, but we do not have a gun. So we borrowed a live trap from a neighbour. The trap was unused and the instructions were still inside it, sealed in a plastic bag. We lugged the trap inside the house and set it by the woodstove for study. I tried to open the trap to get the instructions. The door was latched. I tried, using wiener tongs, to reach through the galvanized bars and pull out the instructions, which would explain how to open the trap. I couldn't do that, either. I picked up the trap and shook it. Still nothing. The instructions in the humane trap were sealed in so well that you needed to be of super-humane intelligence to get them. In my rising anger I thought of biting the trap, or the people that made it. It even crossed my mind that the whole thing was a test of sorts, one of those tricky university studies. Nine out of ten men, when faced with a problem, will chomp it.

I should say here my frenzy was aggravated by something that had happened to me earlier that day. Lily is supposed to start kindergarten next fall, so I had tried registering her for public school. After I filled out a bunch of papers in the school office, a secretary asked if I had Lily's birth certificate.

"No," I said. "I can tell you how old she is. I'm her dad."

"I'm sorry," was the reply. "A birth certificate is required."

In a rush, in a headlong assault, everything that is wrong with schools—from slavish devotion to desks in long tidy rows, to the fart-infested air of an after-lunch classroom, to the bell curve—came thundering down on me.

A birth certificate? When I, the farmer who planted the seed, so to speak, is standing here in blue jeans and a home-made wool hat? Not a wonder home schooling is on the up. That night, after setting the raccoon trap under some hay, I dug Lily's birth certificate out of a drawer, and went to bed.

I knew we had caught something in the trap the next

morning because our cat was sitting in front of it, making faces. As I approached I could hear angry snarls.

What I saw when I uncovered the trap, and the raccoon in it, was enough to explode the concept of humane traps. Humane traps are made by reasonable people who, if sentenced to jail, would learn Japanese, exercise and improve themselves. Confined wild animals only self-destruct. The raccoon we caught had chewed at the galvanized steel bars so intently that the front left quarter of its mouth, extending to its nostril, was open and bleeding. Its claws were raw from scraping.

Lily and I put the trap in the truck and drove to rough forest five miles away. We sprung the raccoon and it scrambled awkwardly up a hemlock. On the way home, we stopped at the school and presented them with formal proof of Lily's age. They set the agenda for the next thirteen years of my daughter's life with the poetry of a rubber stamp. Thud.

Thus, in the span of a single morning, a trapped creature was set free, and a free creature was trapped.

Meaningful Measurements

Some years back, when I was living in Victoria, I had a garden. It was wedged onto the rocky outcrop at the back of our small yard. Four boxes, each four feet by four feet, just like the best-selling square-foot garden book said.

I would come home from the magazine where I worked (in a four-foot by four-foot cubicle) and spend hours tweezering out the tiniest weeds and inspecting marble-sized beets, all with the intensity of a watchmaker.

My neighbour at the time was a retired Manitoba grain farmer. Alistair delighted in mocking my efforts. "Evening, Tom," he'd say, forearms on the fence. "Say, I see all *thirty-six* of your beets are up. Going to sell the surplus? Ha ha!" Still, he was always grateful when I passed over enough fresh produce for him and his wife to have a meal.

Then we moved to the country. Gardens out here are so big, a bushel is still a meaningful measurement. We found a large, south slope lot, with soil so rich and black you want to eat it. What a treat that was. No longer did I have to lecture Alistair on the virtues of intense use, or on the wisdom of planting each seed carefully and at minimum spacing and only in the quantity I needed. With a big garden I could toss out such repressive theories.

Carrots. The first year we had the big garden I wanted carrots. Not sixteen, or thirty-six, or progressions thereof. I wanted plenty. So I spread a jumbo pack of Nantes carrot seed, with onanistic delight, in great long rows. Same with cabbage. I love sauerkraut. I had dozens of cabbages. And too much tobacco and squash and too many potatoes and tomatoes and broccoli and cauliflower and onions and garlic. I didn't measure the garden in feet and inches, I measured by whim and whimsy. And we wallowed in surplus everything.

This year, for the first time, I'm having second thoughts about the virtues of large-scale gardening.

One of the ideas of having a big garden was that I could give the excess away, and have people think I'm a good guy. Or maybe I could swap surplus for good homemade beer, since my homemade beer is never good. That worked, until I took my friend Prescott, who makes an excellent English bitter, to the vegetable plot. He quickly realized that he was trading his hard-made handiwork for what amounted to my compost material—all the beets and broccoli I couldn't use. Since that visit the quality of Prescott's beer has nose-dived. I guess he has decided that since I'm giving him the dregs of the garden, he'll give me the dregs of the fermenter.

And that's not the only problem with the big garden. When visitors see the rows of rotting tomatoes and the broccoli that's gone to seed, they think I'm irresponsible. Never mind that my freezer's full, or that rotting produce will make superb soil for next year's crops. There's food there, and it's a damn shame someone isn't eating it.

Compare that unhappy situation with growing a small box garden. A friend comes over. You say: "Would you like some produce?" and pull up six beets. Six beets is one-sixth of your entire crop of beets. She is thankful, not resentful. There must be a moral there: give a woman six beets and you are a friend, give her a bucket and you're a tightwad.

Finally, it seems to me food out of a box garden even tastes better than food out of a large garden. Logical or not, I don't know. Maybe it's all the attention the plants get, the regular watering and weeding. Or maybe it's having a retired Manitoba wheat farmer watching from next door. Alistair did more for those beets than all the black soil on Vancouver Island.

Shearing the Apple Tree

Our cabin sits atop a bluff at the pointy end of a little bay, off a bigger bay. Sounds from miles around are funnelled to our front step: the bass throb of the big Seaspan tugs grinding through the strait, the splash of a kingfisher hitting the water in front of the cabin. Our house is an ear, and the bay an old-fashioned ear trumpet held tight to it.

One of my favourite seasonal sounds is the whine of an outboard motor. The engines are ornery after a winter's lay-up, as are the tempers of the men who try to start them. Sitting on our deck, you can hear the horselike sound on a reluctant motor. *Ptttth! Pttth! Pttth!* Then: "Aaaaagh!"

If the boat happens to include children, they often add their voices. "Dad! Dad! Dad!" they wail. "What's the matter? Dad! Dad! Dad!"

From where I sit, in the sun, in an unmotorized, reliable wooden chair, it is sometimes possible to hear Dad's thoughts, as he balances the benefits of throwing the kids overboard, and leading a childless but quiet life in some inland penitentiary, against keeping his kids and risking a heart attack.

Our last few days, however, have been fractured by another sound: the angry voices of a young couple across the bay. They live in a rented shack with a bright blue tarp slung across the roof, which we can just make out with binoculars. I don't know their names, but he's got to be a Rick and we're pretty sure she's a Teresa or Terry—a pack-a-day name anyway.

Rick and Teresa moved into the shack last fall. We heard them testing their speakers, and we heard the all-night party that followed. Lorna said our new neighbours sounded like a kind couple, the kind that's either splashing around in bed or hurling pots at each other. She was right. On late fall nights we could hear them caterwauling like breeding cats. It was uncomfortable, for Lorna and I have dampered our own passions, in the hopes of achieving a longer burn.

This spring, all we've heard from across the bay is disharmony. It reached a crescendo two nights ago, when loud music scratched to a stop, followed by shouts. He called her a slob, she said, "Oh yeah, well," and back and forth it went, angry insults flying across the water like torpedoes. Finally a door slammed and she bellowed, "Oh yeah? Well you're just a shitty husband!"

It was a beautiful thing, really. Anybody who loves economy in language would have to agree.

I never know what to do in such circumstances. Something says Go over with a jar of homemade soup and some sage advice, but I have neither. The only thing I can think of is what a neighbour once did when Lorna and I vented differences in public. This was a while back, when we lived on another property. We had a really good, loud fight about something. Then Lorna went inside to knit and I stayed out to prune the apple tree. I pruned it to a stump. It was perform-ance anger.

Afterwards, as I was gathering limbs, a neighbour called over the fence. Did I want a ginger beer? Don was a retired architect. The setup was ripe for a lecture: marriage as cantile-vered bridge, perhaps. But I accepted. Don opened a can of ginger beer and passed it to me. He opened another can and took a long, noisy swig. We both burped and twisted our noses. He opened his mouth, made a sound—like an outboard motor, now that I think of it—then took another swig. Quiet.

When you've been a jerk, there's only one thing worse than a lecture, and that's no lecture. I vowed to myself I'd never fight outdoors again.

Our neighbours across the bay seem to have had a similar catharsis. Last night, all was quiet except for a pair of Canada geese staking claim to the bay. All will be peaceful with them, until another pair shows up.

Antoine!

One of the minor but persistent challenges of country living is keeping dirt out of the home. Clay sticks to the treads of your boots, then sheds in jigsaws on the carpet, or soil wedges under your fingernails and gradually dissolves onto your lunch of cold chicken, garnishing it with bitter grit. At this wet time of year, it seems as if the house is yet another flower bed.

We have two lines of defence against dirt. The first is the Kicking Tree. The Kicking Tree is a second-growth fir near the back door. Before going inside the house, we put a hand against the tree and tap and bang our boots to knock free any clods. We've done this for so long the tree bark is worn smooth, like a rubbing post in a field.

The second line of defence is the memory of a man named Antoine Larsen. Antoine was a very deaf, very dirty Scandinavian farmer who lived across the road from my parents' farm in Groundbirch. He lived by himself, in an unpainted clap-board shack with no power, no phone and no bars of soap.

Most people called Antoine the Whispering Swede. The Whispering Swede's conversation alternated between hush and bellow. His mouth contained a half dozen blackened tooth stumps, and one ball of snoose. This snoose either sprayed over you when he talked, or it dribbled out of the sides of his mouth and ran into the deep creases in his skin. These creases met under his chin, and the snoose trickled in a dirty stream to his walnut-coloured Adam's apple, where it briefly parted, like a creek splitting around a boulder, then reconverged before disappearing into several layers of grimy underwear. During the long northern winters, one of our favourite pastimes was contemplating the snoose stream's eventual destination.

Antoine's position in the community was that of self-appointed consultant. He would appear unannounced—on foot, for he didn't drive—and offer advice on fencing or building haystacks. One of his favourite subjects was land clearing. The way to clear land, Antoine said, was to wait for the dead of summer, then set the forest ablaze. If the fire spread to another farmer's forest, then that was just one of the good turns farmer folk did for each other.

Another of the Whispering Swede's favourite subjects was my grandmother, who came to visit us each summer. My grandmother was a fine Vancouver Island lady who could be summarized in one word, "doily." She was well groomed and fond of lavender soaps. The only remotely dirty thing I ever saw her do was light a menthol cigarette off a stove element.

I think Antoine saw in my grandmother a chance to escape the trajectory of his dirty existence. Soil had insinuated itself into his life as surely as his hearing had left it. He had no idea how to rectify either. Perhaps he thought the well-scrubbed woman could help? Soon after my grandmother arrived, Antoine would come schmoozing around, spraying his snoose. She'd respond by blowing menthol smoke back at him, then cutting short her visit.

To a kid fond of dirty old men and clean grandmothers, it seemed like a great opportunity lost to extremes. A little give on both their parts—less dirt for one, more dirt for the other—and they could have been a small kid's dream couple.

Antoine died several years after we left the farm. A friend reported to us that he had collapsed beside the highway, and was taken to hospital. We heard the nurses had to wash him three times—once for the dirt, once for the grime, once for the snoose. Then he was gone.

Lost in the Hay Field

A farm child's experiences fit into four, maybe five broad categories: the Bad Experience with a Large Animal, What Happened When Dad Left the Keys in the Truck, and the universal Getting Lost in a Hay Field. Getting Lost in a Hay Field is an essential part of a rural childhood, a rite of passage. It happened to my father, it happened to me, and two days ago it happened to Lily.

Lily and I were working in the garden of a neighbouring farm. I needed some drainpipe from a barn on the far side of a twenty-acre hay field. To get to the barn you can either walk through the field, currently full of waist-high grass, or drive around the field on a road. I needed to drive. Lily said she'd rather walk. "I can do it," she said, confidently. "I know the way."

It took me several minutes to drive around and several more to load the pipe. As I slid the lengths of pipe into the truck I glanced at the field, hoping to spot Lily making her way. I didn't want to undermine her independence by going after her too soon; on the other hand, I didn't want a kid hopelessly lost in a field. To force myself into a compromise, I decided to count methodically to one hundred.

The count took me less than ten seconds. Then I was into the field, loping like a cross-country runner. The grass was wet and thick. Several strides and my jeans were soaked. As I ran, I thought of the time on our family farm when I had set out alone through a similar hay field. I was trying to find my father, who was working on the other side of the farm. After thirty minutes of walking in the head-high grass, all I could see was more hay. I wasn't unhappy, I just didn't know where I was going (a still familiar feeling, by the way). So I kept on walking, and walking, stopping only to refresh myself with sweet stalks of grass.

It wasn't until my brother found me hours later, still wandering, that I realized the danger I had put myself in. You were lost, he said. He said I might have sprained my ankle, laid down, and been gobbled up by the baler. He said I might have been eaten by a bear. All this was news to me. I thought I had been on a pleasantly disoriented walk, but according to my brother, I had been stumbling on the precipice of death.

What went through my mind as I charged through the hay field looking for Lily was this: Bears. Cougars. Carnivorous deer stoned on magic mushrooms. Bad enough my daughter was in the midst of her Lost in the Hay Field Experience, what if she should have her Large Animal Experience at the same time? Suddenly, the placid hay field seemed pitted with the dangers of a inner city street.

"Lily!" I called, over and over. If being lost can be defined as being disoriented, then it was I who was lost.

I found Lily by stepping on her foot. She was crouched in

the thick grass, looking for a moose coin which had slipped out of her pocket. "Are you lost?" I asked, not knowing whether to hug her or berate her.

"I think so," she said, looking calmly at the wall of grass around us. "Are you?"

Where They Want Us

If our neighbours are united in one belief, it is that they are smarter with their dollars than city dwellers. The belief is born of experience. Wet firewood you can't give away here goes for $150 a cord downtown. Surplus eggs fetch $2.50 a dozen at health food stores. Urban families visiting the Ridgeway Dude Farm pay $20 for the privilege of milking an ornery goat—and are delighted when they get to muck out a barn stall. I've discovered you can even sell manure from the barn: heaped in a garbage bag with a nice twist tie, it goes for a buck a bag—easy. "Oh! What simply lovely manure!" they say, grunting another bag into the Mercedes. "Thank you so much!" No wonder city dwellers are considered bottom-feeders on the economic food chain, an irritating but necessary part of life in the country, like pollen.

We had an especially large infusion of urban cash last week. A Vancouver film production company descended on us to shoot a beer commercial at a local beach. Like most people around here I didn't know about the commercial until taping was ready to begin. I was in the cafe when Dunc, our curmudgeon-in-residence, wandered in and announced this film outfit was looking for bulldozers and backhoes to clear a road from a lane to the waterfront, where a scene was to be filmed.

No one paid much attention to Dunc. They haven't since the spring of '93, when Dunc started layering the inside of his Husqvarna chain saw hat with tinfoil, shiny side up. The tinfoil, he says, keeps out the "bad rays" emanating from the American submarine base in Puget Sound. He says the bad rays are boiling our brains, like haggis in a pot. Proof is all over, but particularly in some of local council's recent decisions, namely one that prohibited Dunc from subdividing his hundred acres of rock into overpriced half-acre view lots.

Tinfoil in the hat is the latest in a procession of superstitions that Dunc has embraced. You could say he was to the superstition born. When his mother was pregnant with Dunc, she was told by a Suffolk-born cleaning woman that she should only look at beautiful things so the child in her womb would be "well-disposed." So she passed the final five months of her pregnancy in the Still Meadow paddock, the one that used to be a daffodil field and blossomed butter-yellow every April. She sat on a log at the east end of the field every day, from 10:00 a.m. to 3:00 p.m., knitting baby clothes and trying to think beautiful thoughts, even when she was throwing up. "Daffodils, beautiful daffodils," she thought, as she deposited a mixture of apple and homemade yogurt on the grassy edge of the meadow. Apples and homemade yogurt were all she could eat when she was pregnant with Dunc, and even they bounced. She ate so many apples that Dunc has always had an allergy to apples, breaking out in blotches that look like dog prints, on all four cheeks.

Where They Want Us

That allergy is why, when Dunc walks into the cafe, the waitresses know to bring him raisin pie. Last week, after Dunc had squared himself to raisin pie, like a chess player to a chessboard, he mentioned the rumoured budget for the beer commercial: half a million dollars. Dunc said he had seen a goodly portion of the half-million himself, in form of a wad of hundred-dollar bills in a producer's pocket. "It was this big," he said, his hand spread wide enough to hold a Happy Valley onion.

That kind of visual can have a remarkable impact. There was a collective dilation of nearby eyeballs. Within forty-five seconds every single man at that table had downed his coffee, paid, and was backing his truck aggressively out of the parking lot. "Kind of reminds you of spring grass going through a calf, doesn't it," said Dunc, taking a forkful of raisin pie. I've always admired Dunc's way of putting things.

"So, why aren't you out there goosing those film guys for all they're worth?" I asked. Dunc tilted the sugar dispenser over his coffee and counted to five, moving his lips. "They have a half-million dollars to make an ad," he said. "They sell watery beer for $16 a case. And we think we're doing the goosing? Who's kidding who?" It was such a remarkably clear bit of thinking that it made me wonder if there isn't something behind the tinfoil thing.

Dunc went on that day to prophesize that the film deal wouldn't be such a windfall, despite that big roll of bills. A week later, I can declare him correct. Sure, some guys are claiming they made money, but they do that all the time. Miles Watson, who has a small excavator, said he made $3,500 pushing out a clearing for the film site, then confessed his excavator had bust a shaft and it was going to cost $3,700 to fix. Ken Arnold shelled out $1,100 on new tires for his 1977 Ford gravel truck, in the hope he'd cash in, but never got the call. Now he's looking for work to pay expenses for the job he didn't get.

Neither Ken nor Miles fared as poorly as Gina Henry (who, as far as we can tell, is no relation of mine). Gina heard about the film from her husband Dan, who was at the cafe when Dunc broke the news about the beer commercial. Dan drove home and told Gina, and both of them went down to the film site looking for labourers' work. The film union had labouring locked up, but the assistant producer, a pony-tailed woman named Stacey, said they were looking for a tow truck to stand by, in case a vehicle got stuck or needed a jump-start. Gina's dad Giles, owner of Giles Towing, has a purple 1975 Dodge 1-ton tow truck that he keeps for a spare. It pushes a little blue and the radiator leaks, but in bull low the Dodge will pull a small Gulf Island. Gina has run the Dodge before. In fact, that's the truck Gina learned to tow in, and she towed some terrible wrecks, including one on Suicide Corner that killed her cousin Nick.

Gina worked out a deal with Stacey where, for a flat rate of $25 an hour, she'd be on standby. Gina packed a loaf of bread, some bologna and her youngest son Earl, and took a position on a gully above the beach. All they had to do was sit and wait. While they waited, Gina did the math. Twenty-five dollars an hour times three days of twelve hours each was $900. Nine hundred dollars is a lot to a family that hasn't seen regular work since the last snowstorm. Sometimes a Winnebago lumbered past and Gina wondered what kind of celebrity it housed. She had heard that Danielle Steele was going to be in the ad, but that didn't seem right.

To pass the time Gina and Earl, who is twelve years old, played checkers or Go Fish, or they tuned into one of the Seattle FM rock stations. When it got cool they threw a football back and forth, or ran the engine until warm air from the heater displaced the chill in their feet. The only thing they had to watch when they ran the truck was the radiator. Two or three times a day Stacey took a plastic yogurt container, dipped water from the creek in the gully and poured it into the radiator. They slept a lot.

At 10:30 in the morning of the second full day, Earl told Gina that he was bored and was going to play in the stream. Gina said OK, but told Earl not to wander out of earshot. While Earl was playing, Gina thought about the $900 again. Some people dream about what they'd do with a million dollars, but Gina was happy dreaming about $900. She'd be able to get the family car insured for a whole year, instead of quarterly, or she'd be able to get the dryer fixed, so laundry wasn't hanging around the woodstove on ropes strung from table to brick, and brick to table.

While Gina was ambling east in her daydreams, Earl wandered west in the bush. It was later determined he wandered up and over a knoll, though you'd think a kid would head downstream, following a stick ship or making dams. When Gina noticed Earl wasn't around, she hollered for him three times. Then she drove as fast as she could to the film site, told Stacey her son was lost, then drove back fast. At first several union labourers, guys with titles like grip and second grip, came back to help her look for her child. When they couldn't find the boy, the whole film crew shut down and came to look. Long-haired men with fat asses and black jeans fanned out, sweeping through the bush and calling "Earl! Earl!" It was a sight the forests of Metchosin haven't seen since 1931, when the steamer *Empress of the Pacific* went aground at Rocky Point and all the passengers, including members of the royal family of Siam, disembarked onto the shore and made their way to a logging road, dragging silk robes through salal and miner's lettuce.

The film crew looked for three hours before they found little Earl. He had tumbled into a crevasse. He was scratched and cold but otherwise OK. In the short term his worst injury was to his dignity, because he had crapped his pants. The searchers tried to pull Earl out, but every time they heaved, Earl moaned. His left foot was stuck, he said. One of the search party, a slim cameraman, tried going into the crevasse head first to twist Earl's lodged foot, but he could only stretch as far as the boy's knee.

While several men comforted Earl, and even told him a couple jokes his mother later wished they hadn't, several other crew fetched Gina. She was too chesty to get into the crevasse. The only person who was small enough was the assistant producer, who had a boy's physique. With a rope lashed around her waist, Stacey was lowered down head first. When she reached Earl, she said, "If I smile when I'm upside down, it's going to look like a frown, but it isn't really a frown." Earl laughed. Nobody heard this, and Earl only told it to his mother several days later. Then she told it to me.

Dislodging Earl from the crevasse was a matter of turning his jammed foot sideways. Stacey locked hands with Earl, and the grips and second grips with the fat asses pulled the two out of the crack. Earl cleaned himself by the beach, then dressed in spare warm-ups someone found in a van. Everyone had a big lunch. Afterwards Gina returned to the tow truck. It wasn't running. The ignition was still turned to On, and the engine was very hot. In her panic, Gina had left the Dodge running. The engine had overheated so badly it warped the block. Gina had to phone Giles to come and tow the tow truck, and give them a ride home. The tally for the "good deal" of working on the film site was: a traumatized little boy, a warped engine, and $400, that being the amount Gina was paid for her work on the film site.

Where They Want Us

All this has slotted perfectly with Dunc's predictions. He's been patting himself on the back with both hands ever since. "See," he said, when I saw him yesterday, "you're not going to goose those guys from the city. They walked in here and had the whole community on standby, all for a few thousand bucks. Why, it's as bad as what they've got you doing, gift-wrapping cow poop, and all for a measly buck a bag.

"Truth is," he said, "we got them right where they want us."

Part Four

Dog Days

The Parable & the Chicken

Several weeks ago Frank, a woman I work for, gave me a recipe for soup stock. The recipe was printed in blotchy blue ink on lined notepaper torn from a pad. She put the paper on her steps and put a rock on the paper—the same rock she always uses to anchor the many messages we pass back and forth when our schedules do not overlap. I noticed the message in the morning and read it at home after dinner.

Frank's recipe called for three whole free-range chickens, plus a wheelbarrow of spices and herbs. Plucked, cleaned and boiled in a big pot, the chickens made for an aromatic and hearty broth. Frank finished by saying that should I get hold of a few birds, she could show me a nifty method of killing them.

Yesterday I saw that nifty method. Not on an actual chicken, because Frank doesn't keep chickens any more. But on a bag of Uncle Tom's Converted Rice, which was almost as graphic. Frank had just returned from shopping and reached for the nearest package to demonstrate.

"You grab a chicken by the legs and lie it flat, like this," she said, slapping the bag on the gravel. Frank's got the arms of a woodcutter, and in her heyday could wrestle an ornery ram. "Then you put a stick over its neck and hold the stick with your foot, like so." She laid a piece of cedar kindling across the bag and placed her foot on it. "Now, just grab the chicken and *reef up!*" As she said *reef*, she flipped the bag double. She glanced at me to see if I comprehended. I nodded. "No blood," she concluded, "just a broken neck. Now, help me with those bags of groceries, will you?"

Frank's tip is just the latest of many I've received since getting my flock. Everyone has something to say about chickens, even if they don't know a vent from a wattle. Everyone, I now think, has a chicken story in them, just as everyone has a book in them. Basically, advice on chickens comes in one of two forms. Textbook, or parable. Textbook advice is cold and efficient, like Frank's.

Another woman I work for, also the textbook type, used to raise several hundred chickens and sell the meat. This was twenty, maybe thirty years ago. Mary and her husband did it on a scale that warranted a production line. Her husband would cut off their heads, Mary would dip the bodies in a tub of scalding water heated over a wood fire and they would both hang the carcasses on the clothesline for plucking. Mary and I were in her yard when she told me this story, beside the very clothesline they used. "It must have looked like it had snowed," I said, imagining drifts of feather against the ivy. Mary tilted her head and thought for a moment. "No, not really," she said, "It looked more like chicken feathers."

The other type of advice on the flock comes in the form of parable. Parables, I've noticed, are told by people who have been around chickens, but not involved in the actual day-to-day feeding and watering and sluicing out the coop. A chicken makes a useful vehicle for the telling of another story.

Days after we got our first flock, Dave arrived to see how they were settling in. He inspected the coop, stuck his toe in the shavings and said, "Don't forget to shut the door." Chicken coops need to be locked up at night. Otherwise mink, otter and/or raccoons get in and wreak havoc.

I knew this, and said so. But Dave felt compelled to carry on with his story. He used to have chickens, he said. His wife did the actual tending, but he enjoyed having them around. He especially liked one old hen, who survived the rest of the flock. She used to follow him around the workshop, claws clicking on the concrete floor. He'd even let her root around in the cab of his pickup and peck bits of sandwich or burger.

One evening Dave forgot to shut the door to the coop. Shutting the door was his chore as he was usually the last one home for dinner. Later that night he remembered the door, and the hen that was supposed to be behind it, but by then he was in bed and his feet were toasty. Dave did not know it, but entire fortunes have been lost, political dynasties overthrown, empires forsaken, all for the sake of toasty toes. From the seductive comfort of his bed, Dave decided that the hen would probably be OK.

The hen wasn't OK. In the morning Dave went to the coop and found a raccoon. It had dismantled that old hen and was feasting. Dave shot the raccoon—"blew it away," as he says— but the guilt lingers, holding the memory like a stone. There was no doubting the meaning of his parable.

Do I need to say that since Dave told us that story, we have never once forgotten to shut the door to the coop?

Frank, Joe, WAC & Me

With the departure of a large male raccoon from our attic last week, there are now six of us in this cabin. Lorna, me, Lily, Sleeping Cat and two characters we call The Kids. The Kids are Lily's imaginary buddies. Winsome, flighty creatures, they are nonetheless responsible for a disproportionate amount of mess in the home. Just this morning a flat of paints was left open on the floor. In a pre-coffee stupor I stepped on the paints, leaving an imprint resembling traffic lights on my Father's Day Levis wool sock.

"Hey!" I said. "What's this doing out?"

Lily shrugged. "The Kids," she said, sounding more disgusted than me. "And I asked them to put it away, too."

We live miles from Lily's nearest playmate. Friends from the city marvel at this, and speculate how the space and solitude will fertilize Lily's imagination. Lack of socializing, they think, will send her roots deep, just as a lack of water does with plants.

I wonder, though. An imagination is an unsupervised place. I wouldn't dream of setting Lily loose in a mall, to hang out with whom she pleases. Yet it's OK to roam free with characters of her own making? Who is to say she won't take up with miscreants and reprobates? Like Frank and Joe.

Frank and Joe were my imaginary buddies. They appeared when my brothers were at school, my father was in the fields and Mom was in one of her moods. I'd be idling in the dirt pile when, from across the farm yard and behind the granary, there would come a whistle. It was a loud two-toner, that whistle, the type that could summon a mean dog or halt a hockey scrimmage. At the same time I got up, Frank and Joe ambled around the corner.

Ideal characters these guys were not. You could tell by their appearance. Frank was brown and bony and he slouched. His gums had one tenant, a yellowed incisor that leaned like the Wheat Pool grain elevator in Groundbirch. He smoked hand-rolled cigarettes that dripped smouldering tobacco onto his vest. When he lit one of these cigarettes, it momentarily burst into a large flame that left a black smudge on the underside of his once-white cowboy hat. He'd found this hat at the Williams Lake Rodeo, where he had won the Champion of the Known Universe riding competition four years running. He found it the day his bronc-busting career ended. He was walking down the sidewalk when the hat glided past on the street, as soundlessly as a curling rock on clean ice. Frank chased the hat past Lee's Laundry, past Marlene's Fashions & Boutique, until it stopped in front of the Cariboo Gospel Church. Frank stepped into the street. Just as he bent down, a bakery van came around the corner and clobbered him from behind, breaking both of Frank's hips and tearing a rubber band-like thing in his left knee. The broken hips, he said, ruined him— for riding and religion. Now his idea of a good time was to smoke and spit and drink the black dirt coffee I made in a plastic bucket.

Joe was more robust than Frank, with a global face perched over a global belly that his jean jacket was stretched to contain. He looked like a snowman with high blood pressure. The reason for this was that he lived for cheeseburgers and vanilla shakes. He had to have one of each every day. Joe and me saw eye to eye on one thing: neither of us liked red relish on our cheeseburgers. We always scraped it off with the funny pickle they give you in restaurants. Joe wasn't as smart as Frank, which isn't saying much, but that didn't matter to me. You don't keep company with guys like Frank and Joe for their witty repartee.

The three of us were close, but in the way that blackberries and nettles are always close. We were prickly.

"Why, you're so skinny you don't even cast a shadow!" Joe would say to Frank.

"You're so dumb you couldn't pound sand down a rat hole," Frank would reply.

"Both of you shut your holes and get to work," I'd say.

How Frank and Joe made their living wasn't clear, perhaps because the way my family made a living, or was going to do so in the foreseeable future, wasn't clear either. Hence Mom's moods. What I did know was that Frank and Joe were itinerant workers. They trucked bananas to Alaska, ploughed fields and dug ditches, never finishing one job before moving on to the next. Always, they worked in a teeth-clenched panic.

"Dammit, Joe!" Frank would shout. "The burgoyne is bust on the harrows!"

"Dammit Frank!" Joe would holler back. "We better go have ice cream!"

The one chance Frank and Joe had at getting ahead, they blew. This was when they won a contract to maintain the section of the Hart Highway between Dawson Creek and Chetwynd. Highways maintenance was extremely competitive in those days, and each July Highways Minister Phil Gaglardi and Premier W.A.C. Bennett travelled the province in a blue Parisienne convertible, inspecting the roads. Gaglardi drove and Bennett sat in the back, eyes shaded by a black fedora that never blew off. They inspected all the highways in BC, then awarded to the best road crew a fully paid trip to the PNE.

Frank was at best lackadaisical in his attitude to road maintenance; Joe was steadfastly indolent. They filled wash-outs with logs and other impermanent material; they tossed garbage into the Kiskatinaw River. When the Premier and Gaglardi arrived for inspection, Frank and Joe invited them on a fishing trip to Cold Brook, in the community pasture. They said the Premier was a big man to have in your daydreams, and he was to be treated well.

Frank and Joe and Gaglardi and Bennett and me drove to the community pasture in the Parisienne. The air was dry and we could taste road dust on our lips. The dust coated our eyelashes, too, and gave us an effeminate, powdered look. When we arrived at a place called the Pools, the Premier walked down to the brook to fetch a drink, twisted his ankle on a boulder, and fell in. His fedora floated away and even though Frank was closer, Joe had to wade in after it because Frank said his hat-fetching days were over. Queen Elizabeth could drop her tiara in Cold Brook, he said, and the whole damned Royal Air Force couldn't make him get it. While Premier Bennett dried, I made coffee in the plastic bucket. Then Joe tried to show Gaglardi how to fly-fish. On Gaglardi's second back cast, the hook, a sticky-sharp #3, stuck in his cheek. There was no way to get it out because it was barbed, so we packed our uneaten chicken sandwiches and dumped our coffee and drove to the hospital at Dawson Creek.

While we were driving, the Premier made some disparaging remarks about the state of the local roads. They were awfully bumpy, he said. And the ditches, they were full of weeds. "Don't you think so, Phil?" he hollered to Gaglardi in the front seat. Phil responded by clenching the steering wheel so firmly his knuckles turned white.

At the Dawson Creek hospital, Dr. Mather removed the hook from Gaglardi's cheek and patched the cut with two band-aids in an X. Gaglardi met us in the waiting room and we walked to the parking lot. No one said anything. As the two were getting in the car, Frank did something desperate. He offered them $100, cash, to overlook the troubles. The two politicians, after only a moment's conference, said it was an outrage. Then Bennett leaned over the edge of the car and motioned us to come close.

"You god-damned Jesus Christ peckerheads won't ever work in this province again." Thirteen words you won't find in any history book, spoken by the man who built British Columbia.

Then Gaglardi started the Parisienne and they drove off. Frank and Joe and I watched until they were a speck on the history books.

A couple of guys who smoked and bribed politicians? Such characters make me think Lily and all her time alone may not be such a good idea. Against that, though, is a niggling thought. A kid needs friends who back her up—whether she left the paints open or not.

Some time after the incident with Bennett, I got hell at dinnertime for running the well dry on our farm. Afterwards I sulked outside to talk it over with Frank and Joe. "Mom and Dad shouldn't say those things to me," I sniffed.

Frank and Joe agreed, as always. "You're damn right,

Tom, you're damn right." Frank commiserated further: "They probably made you eat mixed vegetables, too."

There will be plenty of time for Lily to form friendships; there's less time for her to actually make them. We'll just have to learn to live with The Kids.

Machinery Grotesque

When I purchased my Toyota pickup three years ago, the former owner loosely guaranteed (with emphasis on loosely) that it would run for eleven months. After that, he said, who knows? The truck was already twenty years old. The unusual length of this guarantee made me think of a fuse, and I expected that on the designated minute of the designated day, the truck would explode, or collapse. Many, many loads of sand, firewood and horse manure later, the truck is still running, though in a way that suggests the end is looming. The engine is incontinent, oozing so many fluids that the parking area in our driveway is forever poisoned, even to dandelions. The body has a skin disease. Some nonessentials, like the parking brake, fell off long ago, and I now carry a wedge of wood to kick behind a tire when I park.

I like the truck. It has been faithful in a characterless sort of way. Yet I wish it would die, so that I could say, "There, it's done." I wish the former owner had been right. There is something offensive about machines that will not die. Their endurance is creepy, like the twitchings of a headless bug. Proper life requires death.

Last fall some friends of ours bought three piglets. Over winter the piglets fattened on garden leavings. Every time we drove by and saw them rooting, we felt better for it. They grew. Then one day the pigs were gone. Their story won't ultimately be much different than my own, except I smoke while I'm alive and they are being smoked after slaughter. It's beginning, middle and bacon.

Machines adhere to a less tidy narrative. Take, for example, an old chain saw that sits in the bone yard. It was made in Germany, though it has had so many haywire additions that it would be more correct to say it is of Germanic ancestry. I bought it for my father a decade ago, to replace a saw of his that I drove over. Several years later he gave this saw back to me. It has cut many cords of wood. It was rebuilt once, after I felled a fir tree on it. The man at the repair shop suggested cremation, but I could not at the time afford a new saw. He installed a new piston, which is like putting the heart of a fifteen-year-old into the body of an eighty-five-year-old. The new engine has enthusiasms that the rest of the saw cannot handle. It wants to shake itself apart. It should be thrown away. Yet to throw out a functioning piece of machinery is to stir up the same thorny questions that euthanasia raises. Should a machine be discarded, just because it no longer functions as well as it once did? So what if it requires twenty pulls to start instead of two?

Such are the challenges of owning older equipment. Most landowners around here dodge the question by parking old machinery in a field, or heaping it in the garage. Like a suite for the mechanical in-laws.

I'm not going to do that. The next truck I buy is going to have a different sort of warranty. It's not the life I care about, it's the end I want guaranteed. For my truck, and for me.

Learning a New Tool

I have gone back to school. Six hours a day, for the last three days. I'm learning to use a mattock. A mattock is that hefty tool used for grubbing hard-pack soil. It is shaped like an axe, but has a pick point at one end and a curving hoelike blade at the other. In profile, it looks like René Lévesque.

I have not used a mattock before. It is a gap in my education, like grammar and sheep-shearing. So I was only too glad to acquire another skill, on someone else's coin. I looked on it as a seminar, a rural version of the software upgrading course.

The campus for this course was the yard of a neighbour's newly built house overlooking several maple-lined sheep paddocks. The house was built on fill trucked in from the nearby federal jail, where a contractor is demolishing several buildings. The fill is made of busted concrete blocks, woven together by mashed-up reinforcing bar. My task has been to take the mattock and hack through this layer of concrete and iron, and make a hole to accommodate a large plum tree.

You learn a lot about a tool in the moments after you pick it up. The initial swing is like a first kiss: all your senses are alive and receptive. One thing I noticed about the mattock is how well it is designed for depositing dirt down your back when you drive the pointy end into the ground. The hoe end hoists a little load of dirt and, as the mattock reaches its apex on the backswing, the soil tumbles off. Some falls on your head. The rest falls into your pants, and your pants pockets, and the tobacco pouch in your pants pockets. That's a delicate procedure for a twelve-pound implement.

Normally I approach an unfamiliar tool with humility. If the tool existed before I was born, I accept that it has been proven useful and that I need to accommodate myself to it. If the tool was designed after I was born, then the tool has to justify itself to me. Thus I am willing to spend years learning how to use an axe properly, but become quickly fed up with weed eaters.

But it was clear after the first two days that the mattock, designed in the thirteenth century, should have been abandoned in the fourteenth century. There is no grace to a mattock, no balance. The helve is too large to fit in the hands, the shank too heavy to be controlled with the wrist. This tool was meant to be powered by hydraulics, not muscle. Each time I swung the mattock, the mattock swung me. I'd hoist it over my head and have to take two steps back to catch up. In this way much of my time was passed commuting to and from the jobsite, which was this not rapidly growing hole.

There is a secret to using every tool, a way to make it more efficient and easier to use. Yesterday, the last day of my mattock digging, I discovered it. Do not stand up. Stay bent, like a peasant. Dirt fell harmlessly from my back, and I didn't lose my balance. I didn't see the maple-lined sheep paddocks, or the dog in the grass, or the hummingbird at the spirea, or any other signs of summer, but then that's not what these quick courses are all about.

The point of education, it seems to me, is as much to discover what you don't like as to discover what you do like. This is why we have universities: to make sure we really don't like a certain subject, say grammar. It is also why we have tools like the mattock. What better way to love the axe than to hate the mattock?

Wanted: A Five-Acre Idea

The deepest division in this community is between land-owners and renters. Landowners, on the whole, think renters are irresponsible; renters think landowners should give them more room for their vegetable gardens. It is an ancient opposition, like crows and hawks.

Recently, though, I've become aware of a small subclass that exists between landowners and renters. It consists of renters who are considering buying property. Property buyers, I'll call them. I am aware of this subclass because Lorna and I are members. We are looking for something between five and fifteen thousand acres, with at least one apple tree, a kidney-shaped duck pond, and neighbours who don't mind George Jones at full volume. Otherwise, we're not particular.

We decided to seek land one evening while sitting on the couch. I have made lots of decisions sitting on a couch, most of which have fizzled like spit on a hot stove. This one has changed our lives, and we haven't spent a mortgaged dime.

The first thing I noticed was that our landowner friends, who have until now waxed unlyrical about tenants, are suddenly advising us of the wisdom of buying a property with a rental on it. A rent can help pay the mortgage, they say. And here I've been thinking renters were a charity project, something landlords did for the health of the community, like leaving a standing snag for woodpeckers.

The other thing I've noticed: I'm officially greedy. I want a pond, and a woodlot, just to say they are mine. As a renter, I was greedy for those things too. But I wanted them for their utilitarian value: the pond to raise ducks, the woodlot to cut firewood and heat my home. Ownership alone won't heat a house. It doesn't taste good when stuffed with sage and roasted. Seems to me what I really want is a five-acre idea—with an apple tree growing on it.

The last idea we looked at was a long, narrow lot near the local sheep-shearer's home. As I walked the fence line, getting a feel for the land, I looked across the three-plank horse fence into the adjoining property. I wonder, I thought, if we might be able to buy the first property, then make an offer on the neighbour's place. That would be nice. Across the neighbour's property, on an adjoining farm, I could see a barn. I thought I'd like to own it, too.

That's the neat thing about greed. It's infinite, and it's free. As I ambled along the fence, stalk of sweet grass in my mouth, I gathered the neighbouring properties into my bosom, until I was squinting at the far blue hills of Sooke, thinking how nice it would be to own right to the mountains. Then I'd kick everyone off and leave the place to the crows and hawks.

Later, when we heard the price of that particular lot, we

coughed in our hands and returned to our rented cabin. We commiserated with tea and criticism: it didn't have a kidney-shaped duck pond, it didn't have a southern exposure. We know now that finding economical land isn't going to be the hard part of becoming a landowner. It's the idea we can't afford.

Working the Water

When you live near the ocean, as I do, you feel compelled to use it. It's as if all that water were an immense garden, ripe for the picking. I'll be sitting peacefully at the kitchen table, watching passing ships, and a niggling, nagging voice says: "Get out there. Catch crabs, fish, anything!" It's pernicious, that voice. It's the same one that makes me feel guilty every time I look at my unused wine-brewing equipment, or the abandoned yogurt maker.

"Use it!" it commands.

Most of the time I ignore the call to do something on the water by pretending I'm too busy with land-based projects: wood cutting, fencing, hunting in the hayfield for eggs dropped by our beatnik hens. Last week, however, after months of Lily's urging, we borrowed a boat and set a crab trap in the bay.

I've never had luck working the water. When I was twenty-five I took a job in a coastal logging camp. It was summer, and because of the fire hazard we had to be out of the woods by noon. The camp was near good salmon fishing grounds and I suggested to several other loggers that rather than idle our afternoons shooting craps, we should borrow the boss's twelve-foot aluminum boat and try fishing. They, who were wiser in these matters than me, agreed, but on the condition we first go to a nearby marine pub for beer. It took us twenty minutes to run them to the pub. We tied the boat to the dock and went in. When we came out a short while later, the boat had vanished. At first we thought some other loggers who had been in the pub had stolen the boat, and we made threatening noises. Then someone noticed two lines leading from the dock into the water. We yarded on these lines. They were heavy. We pulled harder. Slowly, like an apparition, the boss's twelve-foot aluminum boat rose through the water. There was a bung I was supposed to have inserted in the stern before we left camp. As long as the boat was going forward, water didn't come in. Stop, though, and in it gushed.

I rowed back to camp. Our total catch was a lost day's pay to flush out the engine.

Three years later, a neighbour gave me another aluminum boat on permanent lease. The boat sat in my driveway, scowling like a jilted date, until I eventually gave in. I talked several of my brothers into going shares on a small outboard. "Forget the fish store," I said, "we'll fill the freezer with cod." Cod, I knew, was easy catch. And we did catch cod. Lots of it, two weekends in a row. On the Saturday morning of the third weekend we were fishing alongside a log boom in Burgoyne Bay when I decided the fishing would be even better farther along the boom. I scrambled onto the boom in my runners and grabbed the tow line. There was an eight-foot gap between booms and I had five feet of tow line in hand. I realized this critical discrepancy when I was halfway over the gap, in midair. It was one of those moments when time slows to a crawl, and you are able to review the errors in your life, like buying yogurt makers, or wine-brewing equipment, and sorely wish you had done things differently. Then I said something bad and fell in the water.

It was four days ago that Lily and I set the crab trap in front of the house. For the next three days, through the wrong end of the binoculars, she watched the bleach bottle float. We rowed out to check our haul yesterday. It was a fine morning, and as we paddled Lily estimated our haul: two crabs, six crabs, a hundred million crabs. As we neared, we smelled something foul.

"Wow," I said.

Lily made that gagging sound only kids can do properly. "Aaaaaach."

An otter had squirmed into our trap and drowned. Its bloated body had floated the trap to the surface. I cut the trap loose and paddled home, listening to Lily gagging.

"Want to weed the garden?" I asked.

"Yeah," she said, "for a long time."

The Perfect Meal

Of all the great meals I've had, of all the feasts, clambakes and whole pig barbecues, the most satisfying meal was a small steak and kidney pie that I ate by myself in a shabby, one-table, one-light-bulb apartment.

The steak and kidney pie had been made by my Aunt Pat. It was the last of a bunch I stole from her freezer one night when I was drunk, when she and my uncle were out of town and my cousins were having a party. With malice aforethought I entered their pantry and opened a fourteen-foot freezer that I knew to contain many steak and kidney pies. I put eight pies in a bag and tossed the bag out a window. Much later, I stumbled out, grabbed my booty and ran.

Why, you ask, would I steal steak and kidney pies from my Aunt Pat? If you have to ask, you've never tasted my aunt's pies. Succulent, stuffed with chunks of steak impregnated with gravy—they were so good I used to eat three at a sitting, one for nourishment and two just to be a pig.

A steak and kidney pie is a sensible combination of wholesome ingredients. So was my aunt. She went to church and was charitable, yet could, when necessary, call her children "shits." She recognized the fraud behind mealy-mouthed truisms like "God is in the details." Her god was a bulk concept. Accordingly, Aunt Pat did everything big: nine children, parties for eighty-five, meat pies by the dozen.

These pies she made in a tile and cedar kitchen at her rural home in Duncan. The kitchen was made for mass production, just as the home was built for many children. Two ovens, enough counter space to play shuffleboard. Aunt Pat ran the kitchen with a camp counsellor's straight-backed positivism. Nothing was allowed to be bad or tasteless; everything was "great" or "smashing." Mediocrity wasn't in her lexicon, or in her pies. Hoisting food from her freezer wouldn't have been in her lexicon either, had I been caught that night.

The day after the party I woke to a fine smell. In the kitchen I found my roommates feasting on my meat pies. "Hey, what's going on?" I said. "Those are my pies."

"Oh yeah?" said one of them, wiping gravy from his beard. "Think about this, Tom. Is it a greater evil to steal stolen pies, or to steal them in the first place? Answer me that." He punctuated the question with a greasy belch.

The problem was too philosophical then, as it is now. All I know is they left me one measly pie. I put it in the freezer and left it there for a day, a week, a month. Eventually it joined a small glacier of frozen foods that I lugged around from joint to joint, job to job.

My Aunt Pat died one September. I was living in Cranbrook at the time, in a second-floor room in a dumpy house heated by the snorty fornications of an unemployed couple below. The nylon carpet smelled of urine. I was working for one of Conrad Black's newspapers, which paid cub reporters $3 a week.

One night, broke and bummed out, I dug into the freezer. Among the green peas and frozen perogies I found the stolen steak and kidney pie. It looked like something from the Franklin expedition.

I heated the oven and put the pie in. Slowly, a warm, generous smell oozed out, strong enough to overpower the odour of the carpet. When the pie smelled ready I removed it, using my shirttails for oven mitts. I sat down at the linoleum table. I put the fork into the pie and raised a steaming cube to my mouth. Succulent, loaded with gravy—and just the right amount of guilt—it was the perfect meal.

Country Kitsch

In front of our house, tucked under the eaves, is a dilapidated wooden wheelbarrow. It is usually heaped with dry alder stove wood, but it may also contain fresh eggs, sweaters, gloves, grass clippers or my daughter's Pocahontas Barbie, which I find each morning in the chickens' nesting box and move back to the house.

I found the wooden wheelbarrow two years ago, upside down behind a heap of compost. I thought it would be a practical addition to our fleet of wheelbarrows, and filled it with soil from the compost box. Its wheel is made of steel and it has a flat spot. As I made my way back to our yard the barrow heaved, as if it had pulled a hamstring. Roll, flat; roll, flat. Soil sloshed out like water out of a pail. By the time I arrived at our house, the barrow contained two-fifths of the original load. I stationed it by the door and it hasn't moved since.

The wooden wheelbarrow falls into that category of rural

tool that is uselessly honourable, or honourably useless. Rusty Swede saws, wood-handled scythes, wagon wheels, oxen yokes. They are all nice to look at but impossible to justify in any practical way. A bit like the lieutenant governor.

I come from Cowichan. In Cowichan the most coveted useless item is the crosscut saw, often seen riding above a doorway or on a barn wall like half a toothy Cheshire smile. It was natural, then, that when I moved here I wanted a crosscut saw. I asked my brother Guy, who is a journeyman scrounger, to find me such a saw. He did, and I mounted it prominently on the garage wall.

Not long afterwards a friend was visiting from Vancouver and noticed the saw. Had I used the saw, he asked.

No.

Was it a hand-me-down from my family—a high-balling, high rigger uncle perhaps?

Well, sort of... but no.

Did I know how to sharpen it?

No.

I had been confronted with my own fakery, just as I had been when forced to confess that I hadn't actually read many of the hardcover books on my bookshelf. The saw is now banished to rust in the bush, near where I found the wooden wheelbarrow.

The trick to collecting and displaying old tools is deciding what's worthy. Our forebears had many tools on their farms. Why is it we never see mechanical chicken pluckers mounted on a porch? Or those stretchers used to wedge open a cow's vagina at time of birth? And what of the future? Will gas-powered leaf blowers ever be neat to ponder?

Actually, my brother thinks they will be. This is the same brother who found the crosscut saw. Guy collects and displays everything, including a long section of railroad track from the defunct Jordan River mine. The track runs from his house to his mother-in-law's. He thinks it looks good, in that classic mining and smelting style of the 1920s. Guy even persuaded my family to work on this railroad. Pounding spikes, hacking out grade. It didn't take us long to get the feel of the 1920s. First it was blisters, then it was an urge to improve working conditions. We unionized. More beer, fewer five-inch spikes.

All this is my way of saying some old equipment cannot make the leap from practical to fashionable. Guy's railroad is overgrown with ferns and moss, too far gone to be revived. My wooden wheelbarrow, on the other hand, is still hip enough to look good carrying a load of dry alder and a Pocahontas Barbie.

Unto the Shadow

My nephew Brian, who is from the Cowichan Valley, recently returned from a trip to New York City. New York City was to be his reward for a hard summer cutting wood and sweating in a sawmill. He hoped to see *Showboat*, check out galleries, exercise the brain instead of the biceps.

Brian arrived by train at Grand Central Station. He disembarked, turned a corner and saw… a rat. The rat was in a display window, slinking around a manikin adorned with several thousand dollars' worth of Giorgio Armani clothing. Perhaps it's part of the display, he thought. Those crazy advertising types.

Twenty feet farther on, Brian came across a businesswoman, also adorned in a pricey suit, spewing on the sidewalk. That's rough, I know, but that's how Brian put it, and he's not given to tall tales or fish stories. "I couldn't believe it," he recalled, safely back at the family kitchen table. "In New York, yet."

The other members of my family, who are older than Brian, nodded wisely. There is a long and honourable tradition of country folk travelling to the city, only to be affronted by deviancy and excess. Even if the big city is only Kelowna.

I'm thinking of Raymond, the son of some neighbours who lived near my parents' farm. Raymond was known to our family as Strawpiles, because he'd always ask my dad, "How's them thar strawpiles, Bill?"

"Good, Raymond," my dad would respond. "How's your strawpiles?"

Strawpiles's parents decided he needed to broaden his horizons. The precipitating event was a barn dance, where he blew the engine out of his Chev pickup showing off to the youngest of the Laveck sisters. It was the third engine he had ruined in the name of romance, the other two having been sacrificed in front of the older Laveck sisters. So Strawpiles was sent, in the company of a more urban cousin from Fort St. John, on a trip south. They got as far as Kelowna, by which time Strawpiles had had enough. Uncontrolled intersections and fast boats with full-figured women in bikinis. It was too much, he reported.

From that point on, Raymond's trip was recalled in pseudo-Biblical terms. Something like: "Hear about Strawpiles? He went beyond the valley of Wes Hobber, clear unto the shadow of Kelowna. Hell of a place. Cheap gas *and* promiscuity. Don't send your kid."

In one variation of the ritual country-kid-goes-to-the-city story, the rural traveller is immensely practical. Stephen, another nephew of mine, took time off from a logging job to visit relatives in Norfolk, England. He'd quit school when he was fifteen, and at nineteen decided a trip to Britain would help make up the missed social studies classes. One night Stephen and an English cousin were driving from a museum to a pub just outside of town. It was dark, and the trip took them through a stand of royal forest pines. Suddenly a little fallow deer came leaping out of the bush. *Wham.* Right into the side of the Mini.

While the cousin inspected the car, Stephen had a look at the deer. It was dead, but not smashed. Point the headlights over here, he called, and he extracted from his pack a large jackknife. The cousin objected. He didn't think the meat edible, and he was worried about an ancient but still active law about the consequences of eating one of Her Majesty's fallow deer. Something about a night in the Thames. Stephen said he was all in favour of royalty, but was more in favour of venison. He set to and treated our English relatives to twelve pounds of flank.

In a letter he received after returning home, they treated him to an inappropriate amount of praise. How frightfully practical! How frightfully adept! they said. He was frightfully welcome back any time.

I talked to Brian for a while at the same event where he recounted his New York trip. "See any shows while you were there?" I asked him.

"Just the ones in the street," he said. "I'll catch *Showboat* when it comes to Duncan."

The Observer Effect

Every second Tuesday, at 8:00 in the morning, Lily and I muscle three garbage pails into the truck and haul them up to the intersection of our lane and what she calls the busy road, where we leave them for pickup.

Garbage pickup isn't how most people around here dispose of their trash. They burn or bury it. "Put it in a hole in the ground," as they say. I'm not averse to those methods: burying it is what happens at the landfill anyway. But when you rent, as we do, it doesn't seem right to chuck your garbage in the ground. We are temporary; our leavings should be temporary too. Better to fork out fifteen bucks a month and keep the landlord happy. Besides, Lily is big on footprints and animal tracks right now, and she gets a kick out of spotting the wheelprints of the garbage truck when we fetch the pails later in the afternoon.

Lately, though, I'm having second thoughts about garbage

collection. I'm having second thoughts about anything that smacks of city living. What with more people moving from the city to the country, and bringing urban habits and expectations with them, it seems to me there's a danger of ruining the very thing we moved to.

There's a name for this. It's called the observer effect. The observer effect means you can't even watch something without screwing it up. It applies to anthropologists studying aboriginals in New Guinea, to pollsters studying incomes, and to city people moving to the country.

Now, three garbage pails do not constitute a meaningful threat to rural life. But they don't do it good, either. A truck drives out to get the pails. It makes noise. It has a big sign on the side. The driver is in a rush, goes too fast. The speeding truck scares people riding horses on the side of the road. Get enough people putting out garbage pails and soon you can kiss your quiet country roads goodbye.

That's just a small example of how a transplanted city practice can change the country. A much bigger example is what's happening to the local economy. The economy determines the character of a rural area. Around here that character can be defined by two things: chicken manure and logs.

Much of Metchosin is farmland, and every year after haying, farmers spread chicken manure over their fields. Chicken manure is full of nitrogen. Nitrogen is good for the grass. But chicken manure stinks, and stink isn't what some city people planned for when they bought a $300,000 home adjacent to rolling farmland. So now there's a move afoot to stop people from spreading manure. No manure, no hay; no hay, no farmers.

Same goes for logging. Because land taxes are rising, landowners need to come up with a whack of cash every year. Many of them do this by selling logs. Wayne, the farmer I'm working for, is one of them: he's selectively logging a chunk of his land right now. Selective logging sounds good, but still creates a mess. One of the neighbours didn't like what was happening to the surrounding forest. He went after Wayne the other day, climbed up on the skidder, shaking his fist and hollering. He said Wayne was destroying the forest. The neighbour is taking the matter to council. Council means paperwork, and you can't keep a farm running by filling out forms. Now Wayne's wondering if he shouldn't just subdivide and be done with the hassle. I wonder how happy Joe Subdivision is going to be when the condos go up, the water main goes through and the garbage cans go out? Next thing you know, he'll want to import street kids, just to complete the scene.

Once you start thinking about how you might be screwing up the country you can't stop. There's the garbage truck, of course. And the daily newspaper. Even this story is a culprit of sorts. I was running late and didn't want to trust the mail to get it to Vancouver on time. So I'm sending it by courier. I've done this before, so I know the van will come roaring in, make the wrong turn up toward the landlord's house, then roar back even faster and scare the chickens on our driveway and send Lily scurrying for my legs. Couriers are always frenzied, which in my mind is the antithesis of country living, and I make a point of appearing as indolent as possible. Just to rub it in. Package in hand, the courier will jump in his van and zoom up the drive, spinning tires and sending gravel flying.

It won't do much to preserve the country the way we like it, but at least Lily and I will have a new set of tracks to investigate.

Outbuildings

Twenty paces out our back door there is a garage large enough to hold our car, a few bales of hay, plus my chain saws and wood cutting gear. Just beyond the garage is a pole-and-shingle woodshed that leans at a funny angle, and beyond that is our chicken coop. The coop is so cute, with its framed screen windows and steep shake roof, that a poet friend thought it was a guest house.

The garage, woodshed and coop are outbuildings. "Outbuildings" is the catch-all phrase for small, ramshackle structures that dot the farms and acreages around here. Often built on skids, they house tobacco cans of salvaged nails, canning jars, pump and toilet components, PVC pipe, rope, tables, chairs, tools—in short, "good stuff."

There are fifteen outbuildings on this property. Four of these have been built or towed in since we've lived here. That's a whopping increase, percentagewise, in three years. Not long ago I said as much to our landlord, Dave, and told him that based on my predictions there would be 116 outbuildings here by 1998; by the year 2006, I said, there would be 1,550 outbuildings. To put that number in perspective, I told Dave that 1,550 outbuildings placed end to end would stretch all the way to Chuck's General Store.

"Good," he said. "Can't have too many."

Farmers gravitate to outbuildings like flickers to snags. Outbuildings require no building permit, and thus involve no visit from a building inspector. There are few things more dreaded on a rural estate than a visit from a building inspector. Inspectors have a knack for making tangential discoveries while touring a construction site. They notice your environmentally friendly septic field is really a two-inch pipe that spews into a creek. Or they find that the moss-covered extension cords looping through the trees to your workshop are not temporary, as you'd declared in 1978.

With an outbuilding there is no permit, no inspector. It is built from whatever material is at hand, using a design no more formal than a notion. This fact is not lost on local farmers. All sorts of structures are built under the label "outbuilding," the most profitable being rental shacks. Farmers rent them to people like my poet buddy, who thinks it is inspiring to live in a building so porous the wind turns the pages of his manuscript.

Outbuildings are an organizing principle on a farm, much as the Dewey decimal system is an organizing principle in a library. Each outbuilding has its specialized inventory. If I want a green glass insulator, for example, I go to the outbuilding nearest the pump house. It has hundreds of glass insulators. If I want a float for a 1940s porcelain toilet, then my best chances are in the building by the Big Fir, where the plumbing supplies are stored.

"But Tom," friends from town say, "green insulators and

old toilets are useless." And I say, "So are a lot of books. Doesn't mean we pitch them out."

A final comment on outbuildings. They are like second homes, nearby getaways. In the country, where it is not possible to hop a picket fence to visit a neighbour, or zip to a pub or cafe, home can become a very intense place. A place where you are, and are, and are. Together at breakfast, lunch, dinner. It sounds ideal and often is, but sometimes after a week of being jammed, even a five-by-eight shack looks spacious. More than once I've escaped from the house to the chicken coop, where I smoke and throw pine cones for a while before returning to the family.

A similar thing used to happen on my parents' farm. One summer my older teenage brothers got so sick of being cramped in with the rest of the family that they set up bunks in a nearby log cabin. The cabin had once been a granary. It smelled like a shoe. At one end was a small frame window so dirty it filtered the sunlight; at the other end perched a narrow wood stove. When lit, the stove periodically belched smoke out the draft hole, filling the room with an acidic smell that matched my brothers' adolescent odours. Along the walls were swayback bunks, heaped with Hudson's Bay point blankets.

Dad bet my brothers they wouldn't last a week come fall. The chinks in the cabin wall were big enough to let a small storm through. One night of subzero temperatures, he said, and they'd be in their beds in the house. But my brothers winterized the cabin, in their own fashion. They stuffed magazines into the wall cracks, laid salvaged carpet after salvaged carpet on the plank floor, and squeezed two comfy chairs between the bunks. With a full-bore fire in the small black stove, it was toasty, if stinky, all winter.

"It beats being cooped up in the old house," they declared, their stinky feet sharing the lone stool.

Outbuildings

Remembering what my brothers did with that granary makes me think there's a future for the outbuildings on this property. In her teens, Lily may find an outbuilding more accommodating than the family home. That would be all right with me. There are worse places for your kid.

Local
Geography

Every September I cut six cords of firewood from a local family's property and stack the wood along the curving rock wall beside their house. It's a small job in the context of our overall bills, but as reliable as late summer westerlies.

Last year I was working on a corner of the family's land that extends up a mountain. It was in a stand of alder on a steep bank above a gravel road. The soil was mostly clay, and working on the bank was difficult and slippery. The compensation was the slope itself: each time I cut a length from a downed tree, it would tumble down to the ditch below. There were sharp granite boulders in the ditch, and three out of four times the impact on the boulders quartered the wood. Then it was only a matter of tossing the chunks in the truck and carting them to the house.

This year I'm working in another part of the property, a small grove of fir and alder standing between the riding ring and a fifteen-acre pasture. The trees in this grove receive a lot of light, with the result that they are very bushy. When they fall they don't thunder to the earth so much as bounce, then sit there seven feet off the ground like enormous hairbrushes.

The ground in this grove is wet and slippery with runoff, but as always there are compensations. To get to the grove I have to go through the horse barn. By the time I arrive for work the horses have already been fed and watered; they greet me with blasts of pungent recycled alfalfa, nostrils flaring like nozzles on a booster rocket. Their breath reminds me of the time I worked in an office, and how I'd be greeted each morning by not-so-pungent blasts from a stable of photocopiers. If they could have installed a horse at the front door I might have stuck it out.

I like the intimacy of working in these little jobs, in these limited areas. Over several days you walk, crawl, climb, slip and sit on every square foot, until it is as familiar as your own body. You trip over the roots, feel the spongy ground under the spring of the axe. It's a natural braille.

At the northeast end of the riding ring a white plastic drainpipe juts sideways out of the bank. A steady flow of really rotten-looking water emerges from this pipe and makes its way through the grove and into the pasture. Most of the trees I felled yesterday were on one side of this little watercourse, but the wood needed to be stacked on the other side. I estimated I'd cross that waterway maybe two hundred times. So I sawed a four-foot chunk of fir lengthwise, and laid the halves side by side to form a bridge. When I crossed the bridge with armloads of wood, my boots went *thump, thump*. I noticed that every time I *thump, thump*ed, a tree frog in a nearby grove joined in. *Thump, thump, reep, reep.* When I stopped, he stopped. Or so I thought. He was probably thinking: this is funny, whenever I make a sound, that guy carries a load of wood.

The Ideal Dog and Other Delusions

By midday I felt so comfortable in this grove, so at home, that I carved a chair from a stump. I collected pitchy bits of fir and lit a fire. Beside the fire I placed an unsplit chunk, to hold my thermos. Then I sat. To rush through lunch in a place like this would be like eating tuna out of the can at home: cheap and disrespectful of yourself. I stayed quiet and tried not to think.

About two in the afternoon I lugged the last of the wood from the far side of the small creek. I pried the pieces of my homemade bridge from the ground, scraped off the mud and bucked them into firewood, to go on the growing pile I was moving farther into the grove. Not far, really, but when you measure your worksite in tree lengths, a few paces is a long way. No bridge, no frog. I was sorry to see them go, but when you travel as far and wide as I do, that's the toll you pay.

View Lot

After three weeks exploring the local real estate market—of prowling through people's barns and peeking into their bedroom closets—I'm willing to make a couple of declarations: 1) there are more weightlifters in rural Metchosin than you can shake a barbell at; and 2) great, sweeping views are overrated and overpriced.

We've seen a lot of chrome and blue plastic weights sets in basements, even in living rooms. And outside these rooms are sloping vistas, with rolling local hills in the middle distance, and the great jagged incisors of Washington state's Olympic Mountains in the background. That's the viewing formula, set on red wall-to-wall.

Metchosin is rugged. To gain the views, houses have been built on stilts; from a distance, the community appears to be on its collective tiptoes, each house peering over a neighbour's shoulder to gain a better view. There seems to me some relationship between the weights and the views. Implicit in each is an overeager quest for the great, the grandiose, the spectacular. "Look at me," they say.

The home we toured yesterday was on an acreage, overlooking Parry Bay in the foreground and Mount Baker in the background. The front of the house was a wall of window. My first thought was we'd have to calculate Windex costs, along with fire insurance and property taxes, in our monthly expenses.

A realtor let us into the house. She showed us the rec room with the obligatory weightlifting gear, and then took us upstairs to enjoy the view. The view was so big, so keen to display itself, that I was reminded of the fleeting joys of quick sex. We got everything in that house, all at once, without even knowing if the septic had passed a perk test. A home with a sense of propriety, it seems to me, wouldn't offer up all its treasures so swiftly.

Later, while I was outside enjoying a post-viewing smoke, the realtor asked what I thought of the place. "Nice to look at," I said, "but not something you'd want to live with."

The trouble with big, muscular homes is that they squander their assets. From the moment you step inside the two-storey foyer, they assault you with views from every direction. Several of the homes we've looked at have expansive views of the Strait of Juan de Fuca. The strait is a beautiful stretch of water, but viewed morning to night, day in, day out, even its magnificence would be reduced to a commonplace, if not a cliché. Better to catch glimpses of the strait from a trip to the woodpile, and keep it precious.

These homes we've been looking at also seem to embody a prejudice for views of the natural over views of the domestic. Who says a distant wooded valley is more stirring than a gravel pit? If it's real stirring we're after, nothing beats a child's toy left in the yard. Viewed from inside the house, on a rainy day, a yellow plastic wheelbarrow lying smack in the driveway can stir you in ways a pristine valley never could.

Yesterday, after viewing too many overwhelming homes, Lorna and I thankfully returned to our rented cabin, the one with the skinny hallway and knobby stairs. We sat quietly, looking out a small window, which framed an overwhelmingly beautiful scene of dandelions strewn with our daughter's rainbow-coloured garden toys. The dandelions won't last as long as Mount Baker, but that kind of view endures.

Fire-tender

For the last three days our cabin has been enveloped in an eye-watering, acidic white smoke. It's the kind of smoke you can taste in the grit under your fingernails, and smell on the bathroom towels. The smoke comes from fires we've had going in the bush. We have five: one in front of the guest shack, three around what we call Lucy's garden, and one that started by the bluff but has since snuck, like an arsonist, toward the old horse shed. I was so worried about that fire I woke last night and padded out there in my dressing gown to check it. The fire was asleep, but in that too-quiet way kids use to fool parents. So I poked it.

Of all the elements, fire is the most lifelike. It hides, sneaks, stinks and reproduces. Which, according to Tom Henry biology, are the basics of life. Fires are also moody, placing them among the Higher Orders.

Fires are our biannual attempt to keep order in our yard:

one in spring, one in fall. All summer the forest rains needles and limbs, and we rake them into great heaps, like beaver dams. By September the wind and sun have dried the heaps enough so they can be lit with a handful of newspaper. Ours took off with the help of a brisk northerly, so the smoke ran low on the ground and burst out into the bay, as if shot from a cannon. And all along the road into town last week, white plumes billowed out of the forest as our neighbours, like us, took advantage of a wetting shower to torch a summer's worth of debris.

There's always a collective pause in the community when these fires take off: the bright yellow of licking flames and a high-rising smudge can mean a good neighbour, or it can signal the construction of yet another house. First the fire, then the carpenters; then, before you know it, someone else is selling free-range eggs.

Some country tasks, like wood cutting or coop cleaning, are never ending. With fires, though, it's a quick hit. You light them, and that's your life for the next few days. It's like having a guest in the house: fires are all you can think of. Our house smells of smoke; our clothes are thick with it; pastel fires have suddenly blossomed on Lily's artwork. "If the sun is a big fire," she asked, "who lit it?"

There's something invigorating about fire. It's like stump clearing or rock picking: there is the feeling of progress about it, a kind of optimism that our forebears must have felt when they cleared the land. It's the first step in taming the wilderness.

I know the energy of it infected the youngest and oldest residents of the property. Lily, age five, and Mavis, age eighty-two, set to the fires with a pioneer's vigour. They dragged fallen limbs from the salal, sometimes working alone, sometimes together, and heaved them into the blaze. My thinking has always been that fires burn best if someone stares at the flames, and that is largely what I did. The most work I did was moving from one fire to stare at another. Around the yard I went, like a window shopper looking at TVs. My biggest problem was smoking: how can you justify having a cigarette when you're coughing wood smoke?

Meanwhile, Mavis and Lily, who averaged out to one healthy forty-three-year-old, heaped up another fire. Yesterday, while they were working and I wasn't, it occurred to me that I'd like to a have a job tending fires. A fire-tender, I'd call myself. I'd have a red truck with a winch on the front and a brother in the back, or maybe two...

Today that fancy is gone. The fires are embers. There is other work to be done. The one fire that remains, the sneaky one, is sending up a lazy smudge, and an easy southwesterly is taking it over Victoria, towards the Big Smoke. I'm keeping my eye on it.